BACH'S DIE KUNST DER FUGE

A Living Compendium of Fugal Procedures

With a Motivic Analysis
of All the Fugues

Adel Heinrich

UNIVERSITY
PRESS OF
AMERICA

Copyright © 1983 by

University Press of America, Inc.

P.O. Box 19101, Washington, D.C. 20036

Library of Congress Cataloging in Publication Data

Heinrich, Adel.
   Bach's Die Kunst der Fuge.

   Bibliography: p.
   1. Bach, Johann Sebastian, 1685-1750. Kunst der
Fuge. 2. Fugue. I. Title.
MT145.B14H27 1983   781.4'2   82-20095
ISBN 0-8191-2866-X
ISBN 0-8191-2867-8 (pbk.)

214256

TO

PROFESSORS BRUCE BENWARD

AND

JOHN HARVEY

iii

ACKNOWLEDGMENTS

I wish to acknowledge the valued guidance of my various Professors at the University of Wisconsin-Madison in the completion of my original dissertation.

First and foremost, Dr. Bruce Benward, whose astute direction in making students aware of the most minute detail of composition afforded many guidelines for the within analysis of Die Kunst der Fuge. I also would like to express my gratitude to Professor John Harvey for his dedicated musicianship leading to the ultimate performance of this work. Professor Harvey's attention to the significance of every phrase and motive within the music performed in the recitals as part of the Doctor of Musical Arts degree opened new insights into analytical studies.

Grateful acknowledgment is given to Professor Robert Monschein, whose classes evidenced superior scholarship; to Dr. Robert Crane, for his excellent support in the initial stages of this thesis; and to Ellen O. Burmeister and Ilona Kombrink, for their sensitive and musical inquiries into the completion of this thesis.

I would also like to thank Mrs. Alice Breider, Secretary of the Graduate School of Music of the University of Wisconsin-Madison, for her patient assistance in the ultimate finished thesis.

A special word of appreciation is given to Deria C. Beattie, a music major at Colby College of the class of 1983. She has served as a Student Research Assistant under a Grant from Colby College to assist in all the final details required in preparing this manuscript for publication. She also meticulously added the coded motivic analysis that was necessary in the transliteration of the original color-coded system as appeared in my dissertation in the library of the University of Wisconsin-Madison.

I would also like to thank my mother, who carefully prepared the original score before it was analyzed.

Each of my colleagues in the Music Department at Colby College offered their enthusiastic support of the completion of this manuscript, and may I include them in this listing of acknowledgments: Professor Peter Re, Dr. James Armstrong, Mrs. Dorothy Reuman and Dr. Paul Machlin.

Grateful appreciation is also given to the Administration of Colby College, who has assisted in numerous ways not only the completion of this dissertation, but the acquisition of my doctoral degree itself.

A word of appreciation is also due the typists of this final manuscript, Karen Bourassa and Mary Farrell, who were so patient in giving care to every detail.

TABLE OF CONTENTS

(TABLE OF CONTENTS, continued)

LIST OF CHARTS

LIST OF MUSICAL SCORES
WITH MOTIVIC ANALYSES

<u>CODE FOR WITHIN ANALYSES</u>

<u>MAIN THEMATIC MATERIAL</u>   MOTIVES

Subject I

Answer I

Intermediate Sub. I

Subject II   From Subject II

Answer II

Subject III   From Subject III

Answer III

Counter-Subject I   From CS I

Counter-Subject II   From CS II

Counter-Subject III (none exists
    other than a previous
    Subject)

New Material   From New Material

NOTE:
The complete color-coded scores can be seen in the original thesis
in the Memorial Library of the University of Wisconsin, Madison.

ABBREVIATIONS USED IN THIS THESIS

Subject	-	Sub.
Answer	-	Ans.
Counter-Subject	-	CS
Exposition	-	Expo.
Section	-	Sec.
Contrapunctus	-	C.
Soprano	-	S
Alto	-	A
Tenor	-	T
Bass	-	B
Measure Numbers	-	M. 1, Ms. 2-4
Motives from Sub.	-	Sub.(1), Sub.(2), etc.
Motives from Subjects in Double, Triple, and Quadruple Fugues	-	ISub.(1)
		IISub.(1)
		IIISub.(1)
Motives from CS	-	CS(1), CS(2), etc.
Chr. M.	-	Chromatic Motive (In C. XI)

PREFACE

The within study was first made for my dissertation for the Doctor of Musical Arts degree at the University of Wisconsin-Madison. This dissertation included two appendices, which have not been included within this book. One Appendix gave suggestions for the performance of Die Kunst der Fuge, approaching each fugue as an individual composition. The second Appendix was a tape of my performance of the entire Work on the organ in the Eastman Recital Hall of the University of Wisconsin-Madison. My performance was meant to illustrate the analyses set forth within this thesis.

Since that time, I have performed Die Kunst der Fuge, with accompanying lectures, in numerous colleges, including at Colby College, Brown University, Bowdoin College and St. Michael's College.

The suggestions for performance are not included in this book because of the inclusion of the detailed motivic analyses. From a study of each analyzed score, together with the accompanying verbal description of each fugue, it would seem the within study could benefit any type of performance, whether it be keyboard or ensemble.

A word is in order about the origin of the within study. The first four simple fugues were the only fugues planned on being analyzed for my doctoral dissertation. However, from a detailed motivic analysis and a comparison of procedures in each of the four simple fugues, it became apparent that Bach's approach to the writing of these fugues was pedagogy of the highest order. It seemed insufficient to leave this study incomplete. Only from an equally detailed analysis of the remaining fugues did many of the insights presented in this study emerge. Because of the awesome dedication Bach displayed in the completion of every component of each fugue, a correlary detailed analysis seemed appropriate out of respect for Bach's pursuit of fugal knowledge.

This writer has the greatest respect and admiration for all analyses made of Die Kunst der Fuge, and learned a great deal from these sources. Without such a complete study as found here, however, the enormity of Bach's profundity in fugal composition could not have been understood.

xvii

The emphasis of this study is Bach's treatment of the fugue form. A thorough harmonic analysis is beyond the scope of this study, and key relationships are suggested only to show their significance to the procedures of the fugue form.

CHAPTER ONE
PURPOSE, HISTORY AND EXTANT EDITIONS

This thesis will endeavor to prove that Die Kunst der Fuge of Johann Sebastian Bach is a living compendium of fugal procedures revealed not only in the form of a theoretical study, but as a musically intrinsic and cumulatively coherent work.

Since Bach was unable to complete this work before his death, many problems exist about this collection of fugues, known today by the title of Die Kunst der Fuge. What was Bach's purpose in writing a series of fugues based on one subject all in the same key? For what performing medium was the work intended? Was the work to be performed at all, or was it merely a study in canon, counterpoint and fugue? Was Contrapunctus XVIII (the quadruple fugue) part of this work, and if so, what was the overall design? In what order did Bach intend to have the various contrapuncti appear? And one last question, how can progeny benefit from the contrapuntal insights revealed in this work when applied to new compositions or analyses of the fugue form?

Because each of these questions cannot be answered without considerable research, and because numerous scholars have devoted many years to discovering the answers to some of these questions, this thesis will confine its study to the first and last questions raised above: What is the purpose of Die Kunst der Fuge and what value can be derived for the composition and analyses of the fugue form? Peripheral attention will be given to the remaining questions raised above.

In the absence of a written intent by Bach for this work, the within analyses will attempt to divulge how Bach meticulously crafted twenty innovatively distinct fugues based on the same subject to illustrate his insights into the potential of the genre of the fugue. Bach did not choose to write a textbook or treatise dealing with various aspects of fugal construction, as may be found in Gradus ad Parnassum, by Johann Joseph Fux, or Abhandlung von der Fuge, by Friedrich Wilhelm Marpurg. Die Kunst der Fuge is rather an idealized musical composition realizing in practice the principles of contrapuntal fugue writing as promulgated by Bach. This idea may have been inspired by Johann Theile in his Musicalisches Kunstbuch.[1]

1

Bach clothes his mathematically-conceived contrapuntal rules in the highest expression of musical compositions in Die Kunst der Fuge. His fugues do not remain in the category of mundane theoretical examples; his fugues disclose the lofty aesthetic and musical standards which are capable of being achieved by following his precepts in fugal counterpoint.

Because each of the fugues is based on the same subject, and because each fugue additively exemplifies new procedures in fugal structures, Die Kunst der Fuge may be viewed as one cumulative work. Webster's New Twentieth Century Dictionary of the English Language, unabridged (rev. Harold Whitehall, Cleveland and New York: The World Publishing Company, 1951), includes the following definitions for the connotation of the word "cumulative": "composed of parts in a heap; forming a mass;" ... "increasing or augmenting by addition; as, a cumulative action; a cumulative argument;" ... "augmenting or tending to establish a point already proved by other evidence;" and finally, "cumulative argument; an argument in which the different proofs are complete in themselves, and, not being dependent one on the other, tend to one conclusion."

This last definition is most important for the contentions in the within thesis. Every fugue in Die Kunst der Fuge offers further substantive evidence of Bach's implied conclusion regarding his understanding of the fugue form: the fugue is more than a scholarly theoretical pursuit for a specific age; i.e., the individual components of a fugue can be constructed in a numberless variety of ways without deviating from rigid contrapuntal rules; the components can be combined in an equally flexible list of procedures without violating the basic premises of fugal construction; and the genre of the fugue is boundless in adapting to new musical theories and styles, while retaining a high degree of musicianship.

This thesis will strive to deduce as many principles for fugal composition as may be uncovered by a thorough analysis of individual components and their procedures in each of the twenty fugues. From a detailed analysis of this type, it will be seen that the fugues are additive in nature. Although Die Kunst der Fuge has been called a series of fugal variations on one theme, it is the contention of this thesis that the individual fugues are more than variant settings. In analyzing each new fugue as a separate collection of

2

fugal components, the cumulative nature of <u>Die Kunst</u> <u>der Fuge</u> is evidenced, since each fugue augments rules for the construction of the previous fugues. The progressive and individual nature of each of the fugues has been pointed out by numerous scholars.([2]) This cumulative aspect identifies the pedagogical intent of Bach.

In the completion of many fugues, Bach went beyond the existing fugue conventions of the Baroque age. He opened doors for progeny that transcended a harmonic idiom. He promulgated procedures for individual components that could be interchanged between various fugue types. The theories set forth by the twentieth century composers Paul Hindemith, with his weighted intervals, and Arnold Schönberg, with his twelve-tone scale, could easily be used in recreating a series of fugues based on the ideas in <u>Die Kunst der Fuge</u>, although the procedures could be combined in different ways from those set forth by Bach. Bach has illucidated basic combinations of fugal components which could lead to an infinite number of completed fugues, all different from his.

An indeterminate set of ideas steeped in strict contrapuntal rules but garbed in the highest musical settings has been molded by Bach in <u>Die Kunst der Fuge</u> to perpetuate the plasticity and inherent adaptability of this form to conform to the evolutionary vicissitudes of musical theory.

In studying and analyzing <u>Die Kunst der Fuge</u>, the knowledge acquired could lead to the following initial goal on the part of Bach. Bach's master plan for the completion of this series of fugues could have been devised along the following outlines:

1) Compose a sufficient number of fugues to expose the viability of the fugue genre as a musical composition;

2) Design the framework for each fugue in varying ways, so that the techniques of exposing the subjects, the intermediate sections, return to subjects, and conclusions, can evidence their latent flexibility;

3) Include examples of the various fugue types: simple, stretto, double and triple fugues, a variety of two-part canons showing their

relationship to the fugue, mirror fugues in three and four parts, and a concluding quadruple fugue;

4) Retain the basic subject for all the fugue types; by changing the character of the subject or elaborating upon the basic theme, the character of the ensuing fugue can change;

5) Preserve the same key throughout; while Mattheson drew relationships [3] between different keys and affections, the change of key is not necessary to produce different characteristics; the motivic and rhythmic content of the subject or theme, followed by a correlative style, can produce many of the same results;

6) Present the germinal ideas in expositions that go beyond the mere statement of the proper sequence of subject, answer, or counter-subject;

7) Seek out new developmental processes for the episodes and free voices surrounding the subject or answer, other than traditional motivic development;

8) Study the function of the coda for not only summation of ideas, but recapitulation of ideas as more extended conclusions and references to the preliminary expositions;

9) Always strive for a high degree of musicianship, to prove that fugal construction need not sacrifice the beauty of its music in adhering to rigid contrapuntal rules.

This thesis will follow the above basic outline, and summarize some of the main fugal procedures as presented in Die Kunst der Fuge: the fugue types, overall design of each fugue, various contours of the initial fugue subject, and analyses of the expositions, counter-subjects, episodes, free material, and codas.

Upon analyses of these components of the fugue form, brief mention will be made as to how these techniques can be interchanged between one fugue and another, or even adapted to new musical theories.

Die Kunst der Fuge was believed to be begun in 1749, but recent scholarship is presenting evidence leading to an earlier date.[4] As a mature work the musical content embodies the highest level of compositional techniques recognized by Bach.

Numerous theorists and scholars have undertaken studies of the fugue form based on Bach's precepts, and have further made analyses of the individual fugues in Die Kunst der Fuge. Friedrich Wilhelm Marpurg, in his Abhandlung von der Fuge, discusses six classifications of fugues according to melodic motion. He further describes each of the components of the fugue separately, i.e., the subjects, answers, expositions, developments, varying entrances of voices in expositions, counterparts, and the episodes. He then discusses elements as chromaticism, entrance on the dominant, and cadences. Within these individual component parts of the fugue form, Marpurg outlines various procedures that can be followed in completing any one component of the fugue. Scholars suggest this work was written by Marpurg based on many of the suggestions found in Die Kunst der Fuge of Bach. Alfred Mann in his The Study of Fugue [5] gives numerous translations of the discussions of Marpurg's Abhandlung.

In 1841, Moritz Hauptmann made an analysis of Die Kunst der Fuge, reprinted in 1861, in Erlauterungen zu J.S. Bachs Kunst der Fuge. Hauptmann analyzes the fugue types with their contrapuntal procedures, and includes basic thematic outlines for the various fugues.

Sir Donald Tovey edited a scholarly edition of Die Kunst der Fuge with an accompanying Companion to 'The Art of Fugue', published in 1923 and 1931 respectively. Tovey analyzes in detail the contrapuntal usages in this work, with numerous references to the significance of the fugal components. He discusses in detail questions relating to Contrapunctus XVIII, composing several conclusions himself. Analytical comments are included in editions of Die Kunst der Fuge by Harris and Norton for string quartet; Marcel Bitsch, open score; Hans Gal, open score; Wilhelm Rust in Vol. 25 of Bach-Gesellschaft; and a brief commentary of Wolfgang Graeser in JG. XXVIII, Heft 1, in Neuen Bachgesellschaft.

Die Kunst der Fuge is listed in the Schmieder

Catalogue as BWV 1080.

Miscellaneous research has been undertaken by
Dr. Erich Schwebsch, among other scholars. Dr.
Schwebsch is responsible for a two-piano arrangement of
Die Kunst der Fuge, and wrote a lengthy treatise draw-
ing parallels and relationships between this work and
the vibrations of the universe. Tovey proposed the
theory that this work needs a prelude in performance,
and gives several suggestions for works suitable as
preludes.[6] Harris and Norton suggest the possibility
that the French influence on Die Kunst der Fuge goes
into the realm of dance.[7]

Since Bach was unable to complete Die Kunst der
Fuge before his death, numerous theories have been
advanced as to the exact order of the various contrapuncti. The Original Edition gives the order of the
first eleven contrapuncti, starting with the four
simple fugues, the three stretto fugues, and the four
double and triple fugues. The positioning of the four
canons and the two mirror fugues with their rectus and
inversus settings has proven enigmatical. The inclusion
of the final quadruple fugue has also been a question.

The order given in the Original Edition for the
first eleven contrapuncti will be followed in this
thesis. Contrary to Sir Donald Tovey's numbering of
the fugues which excludes the canons as fugues, this
study will include the canons as examples of two-
voiced fugues, following the premises set forth by
Marcel Bitsch in his Introduction to his Edition[8];
by Heinrich Rietsch in his "Zur 'Kunst der Fuge' von
J.S. Bach"[9]; and by Wolfgang Gräser in his "Bachs
'Kunst der Fuge'"[10]. Adhering to the discovery
of Gustav Nottebohm that the three themes of the last
fugue can be combined with the original fugue subject,
the final fugue will be considered a quadruple fugue
composition, not completed by Bach, and an integral
part of Die Kunst der Fuge. The order of the twenty
fugues will follow the order presented by Helmut
Walcha in his organ edition, as follows [11]:

THE FOUR SIMPLE FUGUES	Contrapunctus I
	II
	III
	IV
THE THREE STRETTO FUGUES	V
	VI
	VII
THE FOUR DOUBLE AND TRIPLE FUGUES	VIII (triple, a3)
	IX
	X
	XI (triple, a4)
THE FOUR CANONS	
Canon alla Ottava	XII
Canon alla Decima, (Contrapuncto alla Terza)	XIII
Canon alla Duodecima (in Contrapuncto alla Quinta)	XIV
Canon per Augmentationem in Contrario Motu	XV
THE TWO MIRROR FUGUES	XVI (a3), rectus and inversus
	XVII (a4), rectus and inversus
THE QUADRUPLE FUGUE	XVIII

Although eighteen contrapuncti are listed, this thesis refers to twenty complete fugues. The rectus and inversus settings of the two mirror fugues lead to separate interpretations and thus can be considered separate fugues.

J.S. Bach added a fourth part in free counterpoint to mirror fugue Contrapunctus XVI, adapting the basic three-part fugue to a fugue a4 for two keyboard players. Both the rectus and the inversus settings have independent fourth parts added, so that the added fourth part is not treated in mirror counterpoint. The four-part arrangement for two claviers of Contrapunctus XVI will not be included in this study.

EXTANT EDITIONS:

On page 53 of the article in Current Musicology referred to previously in footnote (2), a complete listing of published editions and arrangements of Die Kunst der Fuge is given from the year 1801 to 1967. The editorial procedures, order of contrapuncti, and instrumentation for some of the better known editions will be collated in this thesis.

The primary sources for Die Kunst der Fuge include an autograph copy and the Original Edition with its two separate printings. The autograph copy, known as the "Berlin Autograph", is listed as Mus. ms. Bach P 200 (Deutsche Staatsbibliothek, Berlin), and consists of the main body with four appendices or "Beilagen". All the music is written in the hand of J.S. Bach.

The first published edition, known as the "Original Edition", had two separate printings. J.S. Bach died before he completed the final editorial details necessary for the proper publication of this work, subsequently leading to numerous editorial procedures and order of the contrapuncti in published editions. The first printing of the Original Edition appeared in 1751 with a short prefatory "Notice", and had no sales. Four copies of the 1751 issue still exist. The original copper plates (approximately sixty in number) were prepared by Schübler, whom Bach had selected for the engraving of Das Musikalische Opfer.

In 1752 the second printing of the original edition appeared, with a preface by Friedrich Wilhelm Marpurg (1718-1795). Only thirty copies of the 1752 printing had been sold by 1756. The one hundred and thirty thalers received from the sale of the thirty copies was insufficient to cover the cost of the copper plates and the engraving. C.P.E. Bach then sold the copper plates for the value of the metal.

EXTANT EDITIONS OF DIE KUNST DER FUGE
(including primary sources)

EDITOR	PUBLISHER AND DATE	INSTRUMENTATION	EDITORIAL PROCEDURES	ORDER OF CONTRAPUNCTI
(Berlin Autograph)		Two staves		Three simple Fugues (I, III, II) Stretto Fugue (V) Two Double Fugues (IX, X) Two Stretto Fugues (VI, VII) Canon at the Octave (single voice and resolved) Two Triple Fugues (VIII, XI) Augmentation Canon (early version, single voice) Two Mirror Fugues (a4 and a3) Augmentation Canon (variant) BEILAGE 1: Augmentation Canon BEILAGE 2: Mirror Fugue a3, arranged for two keyboards BEILAGE 3: Quadruple Fugue, incomplete)
Original Edition, 1751 and 1752		Open Score		Four Simple Fugues (I, II, III, IV) Three Stretto Fugues (V, VI, VII) Triple Fugue a3 (VIII) Two Double Fugues (IX, X) Triple Fugue a4 (XI) Two Mirror Fugues (a4 and a3) Four Canons Mirror Fugue a3 for two claviers Fuga a3 Soggetti CHORAL: "Wen wir in höchsten Nöthen sein"

9

EXTANT EDITIONS OF DIE KUNST DER FUGE (continued)

EDITOR	PUBLISHER AND DATE	INSTRUMENTATION	EDITORIAL PROCEDURES	ORDER OF CONTRAPUNCTI
Wilhelm Rust	Breitkopf, 1878 (1875) with Bach-Gesellschaft	Open Score, with no piano reduction	Soprano, Alto, Tenor and Bass clefs; no tempo markings	I-XI, same as Original Ed. XII, Mirror Fugue a4 XIII, Mirror Fugue a3 XIV (Variant to C. X) Four Canons Fuga a 2 Clav. Fuga a 3 Soggetti
Carl Czerny	Kalmus (same as Peters Nr. 218) Piano Series	Two staves	Includes asterisk (as on p. 83), but omits footnote reference as in Peters Ed. Includes tempo and dynamic markings	I-XI, same as Original Ed. XII, Mirror Fugue a4 XIII, Mirror Fugue a3 XIV (Variant to C. X) Four Canons Fuga I per due Pianoforti Fuga II per due Pianoforti, in altro modo Fuga XV, a tre soggetti (incomplete)
Carl Czerny	Kalmus Miniature Orchestra Score No. 160	Open score, with keyboard reduction in smaller note values	Soprano, Alto, Tenor, and Bass clefs; Contrapuncti numbered individually and consecutively; no tempo or dynamic markings	I-XI, same as Original Ed. XII-XV, Four Canons XVI, Mirror Fugue a3 XVII, Mirror Fugue a3 arranged for 2 Clav. XVIII, Mirror Fugue a4 XIX, Quadruple Fugue (incomplete) CHORAL: with 15 verses of Hymn Appendices for Canons and C. X; listings of Themes

10

EXTANT EDITIONS OF DIE KUNST DER FUGE (continued)

EDITOR	PUBLISHER AND DATE	INSTRUMENTATION	EDITORIAL PROCEDURES	ORDER OF CONTRAPUNCTI
Donald Francis Tovey	Oxford, 1923	Open score, with no piano reduction	Soprano, Alto, Tenor, and Bass clefs; includes thematic index; no tempo or dynamic markings	I-XI, same as Original Ed. XII, Mirror Fugue a4 XIII, Mirror Fugue a3 Four Canons XIV, Fuga a 4 Soggetti, with completion by Tovey Appendix A, Choral-Vorspiel Appendix B, Early version of augmentation canon Appendix C, Final totally invertible Fugue (by the Editor)
Wolfgang Graeser	Breitkopf, 1927 (Neuen Bachgesell-schaft)	Open score, with piano reduction in smaller notes	Soprano, Alto, Tenor, and Bass clefs	I-XI, same as Original Ed. XII-XV, Four Canons XVI, Mirror Fugue a3 XVII, Same, a4 XVIII, Mirror Fugue a4 XIX, Fuga a 4 Soggetti (incomplete) CHORAL: with 15 verses of Hymn With alternate settings of C. XV, XII, and X
Roy Harris and M. D. Herter Norton	Schirmer, 1936	String Quartet	Tempo and dynamic markings	I-XI, same as Original Ed. XII, Mirror Fugue a4 XIII, Mirror Fugue a3 XIV, Quadruple Fugue (incomplete)

11

EXTANT EDITIONS OF DIE KUNST DER FUGE (continued)

EDITOR	PUBLISHER AND DATE	INSTRUMENTATION	EDITORIAL PROCEDURES	ORDER OF CONTRAPUNCTI
Heinrich Husman	Steingraber, 1938 (a second edition of 1938 separates the works for one Clav. from the three stretto fugues for organ, and the two mirror fugues for two Clav.)	Keyboard (and organ)	Treble and bass clefs; no tempo or dynamic markings; includes brief table of ornaments at end	1-4, Klavierfugen für Klav. 5-7, Orgelfugen mit Schlusspedal 8-11, Klavierfugen 12-13, Spiegelfugen für zwei Klav. 14-17, Kanonen für Klavier 18, Schlussfuge für Klav, (incomplete)
Roger Vuataz	Hermann Schurchen, Ars Viva, 1950	Orchestra (calls his use of orchestra "organ orchestra"), 26 strings and 5 woodwinds	MM markings	I-II, Two Simple Fugues, normal order III-IV, Same, inverted order V-VII, Three Stretto Fugues VIII-XI, Same as Original Ed. XII-XV, Four Canons XVIa & b, Mirror Fugue a3 XVIIa & b, Mirror Fugue a4 XIX, Quadruple Fugue XVIIa & b, Mirror Fugue for two Clav.
Hans Schurich, rev. by Bruno Penzien	Willy-Müller (Peters), 1944-1952, 2 Vols.	Organ	No tempo markings; but suggestions for tempi in footnotes; offers suggestions for performance of individual fugues	I-XI, same as Original Ed. XII-XV, Four Canons XVI, Mirror Fugue a3, Rectus XVIb, Inversus XVIII, Mirror Fugue a4, Rectus XVIIIb, Inversus XIX, Quadruple Fugue, with Choral Mirror Fugue with added fourth part

12

EXTANT EDITIONS OF <u>DIE KUNST DER FUGE</u> (continued)

EDITOR	PUBLISHER	INSTRUMENTATION	EDITORIAL PROCEDURES	ORDER OF CONTRAPUNCTI
Hans Gal	Boosey & Hawkes, 1951 (Hawkes Pocket Scores)	Open score	Two G-clefs and two F-clefs; preface	I-II, Two Simple Fugues, normal III-IV, Two Simple Fugues, inverted V-VII, Three Stretto Fugues VIII-XI, Same as Original Ed. XII-XV, Four Canons XVI, Mirror Fugue a4 XVII, Mirror Fugue a3 XVIII, Mirror Fugue for Two Clav. XIX, Fuga a 3 soggetti (incomplete)
(Rust)	Lea Pocket Scores No. 73, 1955	Open Score	(From the Bach-Gesellschaft Edition)	Same as Bach-Gesellschaft Edition
Marcel Bitsch	Durand et Cie, 1967	Open Score	Two G-clefs and two F-clefs; MM markings; commentary	I-XI, Same as Original Ed., but organized into three Groups XII-XV, Two-voice fugues in Canon form XVIa & b, Mirror Fugue a3 XVIIa & b, Variant in four voices XVIIIa & b, Mirror Fugue a4
Helmut Walcha	Henry Litolff's (Peters), 1967	Organ	MM markings and exact minutes for each fugue; articulation indications; suggestions for registration	I-XI, Same as Original Edition XII-XV, Four Canons XVI, Mirror Fugue a3 XVII, Mirror Fugue a4 XVIII, Quadruple Fugue, completed by Walcha

13

FOOTNOTES FOR CHAPTER ONE

(1)   David and Mendel point this out on p. 28 of The Bach Reader (New York: W.W. Norton & Company, Inc., 1945, 1966).

(2)   Articles as the following attest to the individual and cumulative nature of each fugue: Current Musicology (Number 19/1975), "Bach's 'Art of Fugue': an Examination of the Sources", pp. 52-53, p. 58; Hans Gal, ed., J. S. Bach, Die Kunst der Fuge, Preface, Hawkes Pocket Scores (London; New York: Boosey & Hawkes, Ltd., 1951), p. v.; Roy Harris and M. D. Herter Norton, eds., The Art of the Fugue (New York: G. Schirmer, Inc., 1936), p. xiii.

(3)   Johann Mattheson, 1681-1764.

(4)   Op. cit., Current Musicology (Number 19/1975), p. 58.

(5)   Mann, Alfred, The Study of Fugue (New Brunswick, New Jersey: Rutgers University Press, 1958).

(6)   Tovey, D. F., A Companion to 'The Art of Fugue' (London: Humphrey-Milford: Oxford University Press, 1931), pp. 62-78.

(7)   Harris, Roy and M. D. Herter Norton, eds., "The Art of the Fugue", The Musical Quarterly XXI, No. 2 (1935), p. 167.

(8)   Bitsch, Marcel, ed., J. S. Bach, L'Art de la Fugue (Paris: Durand et Cie, Editeurs, 1967).

(9)   In Bach Jahrbuch (1926), pp. 1 ff.

(10)   In Bach Jahrbuch (1924), pp. 1 ff.

(11)   Walcha, Helmut, ed., Johann Sebastian Bach, Die Kunst der Fuge (New York: C. F. Peters, 1967).

FUGUE TYPES:

The fugue types can be grouped into five main groups, followed by the quadruple fugue. In Group I, the four simple fugues presented as Contrapuncti I through IV illustrate the possibilities in construction of a fugue using one simple subject with a minimum of stretto devices. In two of these fugues the Original Subject is stated in normal order; in the remaining two fugues, the subject is stated in inverted order. (By "normal order" is meant the original presentation of the subject of Die Kunst der Fuge, as stated by the alto in Contrapunctus I.) The order of entry of the subjects and answers varies in each fugue.

The three stretto fugues in Group II, Contrapuncti V through VII, all have an elaborated fugue subject, which subject occurs later in Die Kunst der Fuge when stretto techniques are emphasized. The subject with normal note values, diminution and augmentation are emphasized in this group.

Group III, including Contrapuncti VIII through XI, draws upon the more advanced contrapuntal writing of double and triple fugues, presenting the Original Subject in combination with one or two other subjects. The four canons in Group IV, referred to as Contrapuncti XII through XV, are included to show four different types of canons and their relation to a two-part or larger fugue form, each canon having an extended subject based on the theme of the Original Subject of this work.

The two mirror fugues in Group V, Contrapuncti XVI and XVII, rectus and inversus settings, illustrate the more advanced contrapuntal procedure of mirror fugue writing, first in three part, and then in four part. The quadruple fugue completes the entire work, presumably included to illustrate quadruple counterpoint in the form of an expanded fugue.

THE OVERALL STRUCTURE OF EACH FUGUE:

Bach transcends the traditional norm of fugal construction by varying the presentation of his ideas in each fugue. The following charts for each fugue, plus brief descriptive analyses, convey the differences

15

in structures. The motivic analyses on the scores
identify all subjects, answers, components of the fugue
and motives.

Each fugue is complete in itself and could stand
as an independent musical composition. Yet each fugue
rigidly adheres to strict rules of counterpoint without
regard to figurations or idiomatic conventions for any
specific instrument or instruments. In some cases,
the order of presentation of subject or answer in the
exposition governs the overall structure. In other
cases, the emphasis on the subject or answer is of
uppermost importance. In no two fugues is the overall
structure duplicated; each fugue additively portrays
a new procedure for the overall structure. These
structures could be interchanged between the fugue
types, and could readily be adapted to more modern
theories.

To be more specific, the subject presented in
contrasting keys in Section III of simple fugue Contrapunctus II, could be a scheme of any fugue type. The
three levels of contrapuntal interest presented in
simple fugue Contrapunctus III could become a format
for any fugue type. The modulations in cycles of fifth
in simple fugue Contrapunctus IV could be included
strategically in any fugue type. References to Baroque
conventions, as the descending third frequently called
"cuckoo" motive in Contrapunctus IV, or the trio sonato
texture in simple fugue Contrapunctus III could provide
contrast within any fugue type.

Chromaticism used for coloration or heightened
tension would encounter no boundaries in fugue types.
Similar procedural ideas in all the fugues in <u>Die
Kunst der Fuge</u> could be interchanged in varying
fugue types throughout this work. In fact, it could be
conceivable that any one of the twenty fugues could
serve embryonic germinal ideas for an infinite number
of fugues within many or all the fugue types.

The four canons have not been analyzed in chart
formation, but have been included with the descriptive
analyses starting on p. 90.

16

OVERALL STRUCTURE IN CONTRAPUNCTUS I
(a4) Ms. 1–78

SECTION	MEASURE NOS.	FUGUE STATEMENT	VOICE	ORDER	STARTING NOTE	KEY
I Ms. 1–23	1–5	Subject	A	normal	tonic	d
	5–9	Answer	S	normal	dominant	d
Exposition, Ms. 1–17	9–13	Subject	B	normal	tonic	d
	13–17	Answer	T	normal	dominant	d
		Episode (1) Ms. 17–23				
II Ms. 23–49	23–27	Subject	A	normal	tonic	d
		Episode (2) Ms. 27–29				
	29–33 32–36	Subject Answer	S B	normal normal	tonic dominant	a d to g
		Episode (3) Ms. 36–40				
	40–44	Subject	T	normal	tonic (e)	d
		Episode (4) Ms. 44–49				
IIIA Ms. 49–74	49–53	Subject	S	normal	tonic (e)	d
		Episode (5) Ms. 53–56				

17

OVERALL STRUCTURE IN CONTRAPUNCTUS I (continued)

SECTION	MEASURE NOS.	FUGUE STATEMENT	VOICE	ORDER	STARTING NOTE	KEY
(IIIA)	56-60	Subject	B	normal	tonic	d
		Episode (6) Ms. 60-74				
IIIB Coda Ms. 74-78 .	74-78	Answer	T	normal	dominant	g to d

OVERALL STRUCTURE IN CONTRAPUNCTUS II
(a4) Ms. 1-84

SECTION	MEASURE NOS.	FUGUE STATEMENT	VOICE	ORDER	STARTING NOTE	KEY
I Exposition, Ms. 1-23	1-5	Subject	B	normal	tonic	d
	5-9	Answer	T	normal	dominant	d
	9-13	Subject	A	normal	tonic	d
	13-17	Answer	S	normal	dominant (altered at end)	modulates
		Episode (1) Ms. 17-23				
II Ms. 23-45	23-27	Subject	A	normal	tonic, modified	d
	26-30	Answer	S	normal	dominant	d
		Episode (2) M. 30				
	31-35	Subject	B	normal	tonic	d
		Episode (3) Ms. 35-37				
	38-42	Answer	T	normal	dominant	d
		Episode (4) Ms. 42-45				
III Ms. 45-61	45-49	Subject	S	normal	tonic	F

19

OVERALL STRUCTURE IN CONTRAPUNCTUS II (continued)

SECTION	MEASURE NOS.	FUGUE STATEMENT	VOICE	ORDER	STARTING NOTE	KEY
(III)	49-53	Subject	A	normal	tonic (a)	g
	(52) 53-57	Subject	B	normal	tonic (c)	B-flat Major
		Episode (5) Ms. 57-61				
IV Ms. 61-79	61-65	Subject	B	normal	tonic	d
		Episode (6) Ms. 65-69				
	69-73	Answer	T	normal	dominant	d
		Episode (7) Ms. 73-79				
V Coda, Ms. 79-84	79-83	Subject	S	normal	tonic	d
		Episode (8) Ms. 83-84				

20

OVERALL STRUCTURE IN CONTRAPUNCTUS III
(a4) Ms. 1-72

SECTION	MEASURE NOS.	FUGUE STATEMENT	VOICE	ORDER	STARTING NOTE	KEY
I Ms. 1 to 23-1/4 Exposition, Ms. 1-19	1-5	Subject	T	inverted	tonic	d
	5-9	Answer	A	inverted	dominant	d
	9-13	Subject	S	inverted	tonic	d
		Episode (1) Ms. 13-15				
	15-19	Answer	B	inverted	dominant	d
		Episode (2) Ms. 19-1/4 to 23-1/4				
Intermediate Section (A), based on Subject of stretto fugues, Ms. 23-1/4 to 43	23-1/4 to 27	Answer	S	inverted	dominant	d
		Episode (3) Ms. 27 to 29-1/4				
	29-1/4 to 33	Answer	T	inverted	dominant	a
		Episode (4) Ms. 33 to 35-1/4				
	35-1/4 to 39	Answer	T	inverted	dominant	F
		Episode (5) Ms. 39-1/4 to 43				
II Ms. 43-55	43-47	Answer	S	inverted	dominant	a, modulates at end

21

OVERALL STRUCTURE IN CONTRAPUNCTUS III (continued)

SECTION	MEASURE NOS.	FUGUE STATEMENT	VOICE	ORDER	STARTING NOTE	KEY
		Episode (6) Ms. 47-51				
(II)	51-55	Answer	B	inverted	dominant (c)	g, modulates at end
Intermediate Section (B), Ms. 55-62	55-59	Answer	A	inverted	dominant	d, altered
	58-62	Subject	S	inverted	tonic	d, altered
		Episode (7) Ms. 62				
III Ms. 63-72	63-67	Answer	T	inverted	dominant	d
		Episode (8) (8-A) Ms. 67-70 (8-B) Ms. 70-72 brief CODA				

22

OVERALL STRUCTURE IN CONTRAPUNCTUS IV (a4) Ms. 1-138

SECTION	MEASURE NOS.	FUGUE STATEMENT	VOICE	ORDER	STARTING NOTE	KEY
I Ms. 1-27 Exposition, Ms. 1-19	1-5	Subject (Same as Answer in III)	S	inverted	dominant	d
	5-9	Answer (Same as Subject in III)	A	inverted	tonic	d
		Episode (1) Ms. 9-1/4 to 11				
	11-15	Subject	T	inverted	dominant	d
	15-19	Answer	B	inverted	tonic	d
		Episode (2) Ms. 19-27				
II Ms. 27-61	27-31	Subject	S	inverted	dominant	F
	31-35	Subject	A	inverted	dominant	C, modified
	35-39	Subject	T	inverted	dominant	g
	39-43	Subject	B	inverted	dominant (g)	d
		Episode (3) Ms. (42) 43-61				

23

OVERALL STRUCTURE IN CONTRAPUNCTUS IV (continued)

SECTION	MEASURE NOS.	FUGUE STATEMENT	VOICE	ORDER	STARTING NOTE	KEY
III Ms. 61-107	61-65	Subject	B	inverted	dominant (f)	C, modulates
	65-69	Subject	T	inverted	dominant	g, altered
		Episode (4) Ms. 69-73				
	73-77	Subject	A	inverted	dominant	d, altered
	77-81	Subject	S	inverted	dominant	a, altered
		Episode (5) Ms. 81-107				
IVA Ms. 107-111	107-111	Subject	T	inverted	dominant	d
	107-1/4 to 111	Subject	B	inverted	dominant	B-flat Major
IVB Ms. 111-129	111-115	Answer, modified	A	inverted	tonic	Begins F
	111(1/4) to 115	Answer, modified	S	inverted	tonic	d
	111-129	Episode (6) Ms. 115-129				

24

OVERALL STRUCTURE IN CONTRAPUNCTUS IV (continued)

SECTION	MEASURE NOS.	FUGUE STATEMENT	VOICE	ORDER	STARTING NOTE	KEY
V Coda, Ms. 129-138	129-133	Subject	T	inverted	dominant	g, modified
	133-137	Subject	A	inverted	dominant	d, ends in g
		Episode (7) Ms. 137-138				

OVERALL STRUCTURE IN CONTRAPUNCTUS V
(a4) Ms. 1-90

SECTION	MEASURE NOS.	FUGUE STATEMENT	VOICE	ORDER	STARTING NOTE	KEY
I Exposition, Ms. 1-17	1-5	Subject	A	inverted	dominant	d
	4-8	Answer	B	normal	tonic	d
	7-11	Subject	S	normal	tonic (ends on super-tonic)	d
	10-14	Answer	T	inverted	tonic	d
		Episode (1) Ms. 14-17				
II Ms. 17 to 33-1/4	17-21	Subject	S	inverted	dominant (d)	a
	20-24	Answer	T	normal	tonic	a
	23-27	Subject	B	inverted	dominant	d
	26-30	Answer	A	normal	tonic	d
		Episode (2) Ms. 30 to 33-1/4				
IIIA Ms. 33-41	33-37	Answer	B	normal	tonic	F
	33-1/2 to 37-1/2	Subject	S	inverted	dominant	F
		Episode (3) Ms. 37-1/2 to 41				

OVERALL STRUCTURE IN CONTRAPUNCTUS V (continued)

SECTION	MEASURE NOS.	FUGUE STATEMENT	VOICE	ORDER	STARTING NOTE	KEY
IIIB Ms. 41-47	41-45	Subject	T	inverted	dominant (c)	g
	41-1/2 to 45-1/2	Answer	A	normal	tonic	g
		Episode (4) Ms. 45-1/2 to 47				
IVA Ms. 47-57	47-51	Subject	B	inverted	dominant	B-flat Major
	48-1/2 to 52-1/2	Subject	T	inverted	dominant	B-flat Major
		Episode (5) Ms. 52-1/2 to 57				
IVB Ms. 57-69	57-61	Answer	S	normal	tonic (e)	d
	58-1/2 to 62-1/2	Answer	A	normal	tonic	d
		Episode (6) Ms. 62-1/2 to 69				
VA Ms. 69-77	69-73	Subject	S	inverted	dominant	d
	70-74	Subject	T	inverted	dominant	d
		Episode (7) Ms. 74-77				

OVERALL STRUCTURE IN CONTRAPUNCTUS V (continued)

SECTION	MEASURE NOS.	FUGUE STATEMENT	VOICE	ORDER	STARTING NOTE	KEY
VB Ms. 77-86	77-81	Answer	T	normal	tonic (e)	d
	78-82	Answer	A	normal	tonic	d
		Episode (8) Ms. 82-86				
VI Coda, Ms. 86-90	86-90	Subject	Bass I (Bass div.)	inverted	dominant	d, altered with picardy third
	86-90	Answer	A	normal	tonic, modified entrance	d, altered as Bass I

OVERALL STRUCTURE IN CONTRAPUNCTUS VI
(a4) Ms. 1-79

SECTION	MEASURE NOS.	FUGUE STATEMENT (with note values)	VOICE	ORDER	STARTING NOTE	KEY
DIVISION ONE						
I Exposition for Subject, Ms. 1-9	1-5	Subject, normal	B	normal	tonic	d
	2-4	Answer, diminution	S	inverted	dominant	d
	3-1/2 to 5-1/2	Subject, dim.	A	normal	tonic	d
		Episode (1) Ms. 5-1/2 to 7				
	7-9	Answer, dim.	T	inverted	dominant ending, begins on tonic	d
II Ms. 8-15	8-12	Subject, normal	A	normal	tonic	a
	10-1/2 to 12-1/2	Subject, dim.	S	normal	tonic	a
		Episode (2) Ms. 12-1/2 to 15				
III Ms. 15 to 20-1/4	15-17	Answer, dim.	B	inverted	dominant	d
	16-20	Subject, normal	T	normal	tonic	d
	16-1/2 to 18-1/2	Answer, dim.	S	inverted	dominant	d

29

OVERALL STRUCTURE IN CONTRAPUNCTUS VI (continued)

SECTION	MEASURE NOS.	FUGUE STATEMENT (with note values)	VOICE	ORDER	STARTING NOTE	KEY
(DIVISION ONE, continued)						
IV Ms. 20-1/2 to 31	20-1/2 to 24-1/2	Episode (3) Ms. 20-1/4, one beat				
		Answer, normal	T	inverted	dominant	F
		Episode (4) Ms. 24-3/4, one beat				
	25-29	Subject, normal	A	normal	tonic	F
	26-28	Answer, dim.	T	inverted	dominant	F
		Episode (5) Ms. 29-31				
V Ms. 31-35	31-35	Subject, normal	T	normal	tonic	d
	32-34	Answer, dim.	A	inverted	dominant	d

OVERALL STRUCTURE IN CONTRAPUNCTUS VI (continued)

SECTION	MEASURE NOS.	FUGUE STATEMENT (with note values)	VOICE	ORDER	STARTING NOTE	KEY
DIVISION TWO						
$\underline{\text{I}}$ Ms. 35-47	35-39	Answer, normal	S	inverted	dominant	g
Exposition for Answer,	36-38	Subject, dim.	B	normal	tonic	g
Ms. 35-47	37-1/2 to 39-1/2	Answer, dim.	T	inverted	dominant	g
		Episode (1) Ms. 39-1/2 to 42				
	42-44	Answer, dim.	A	inverted	dominant	B-flat Major
		Episode (2) Ms. 44-47				
$\underline{\text{II}}$ Ms. 47-57	47-51	Answer, normal	B	inverted	dominant	d
	48-50	Subject, dim.	T	normal	tonic	d
		Episode (3) Ms. 51-57				
$\underline{\text{III}}$ Ms. 57 to 63-1/2	57-59	Subject, dim.	S	normal	tonic (e)	d
	58-62	Answer, normal	A	inverted	dominant	d
	58-1/2 to 60-1/2	Subject, dim.	T	normal	dominant	d

31

OVERALL STRUCTURE IN CONTRAPUNCTUS VI (continued)

SECTION	MEASURE NOS.	FUGUE STATEMENT (with note values)	VOICE	ORDER	STARTING NOTE	KEY
(DIVISION TWO, continued)						
		Episode (4) Ms. 62 to 63-1/2				
IV Ms. 63-1/2 to 74-1/2	63-1/2 to 65-1/2	Subject, dim.	T	normal	tonic	F
	64-1/2 to 68-1/2	Answer, normal	S	inverted	dominant	d
	65-1/2 to 67-1/2	Subject, dim.	A	normal	tonic	d
		Episode (5) Ms. 68-1/2 to 74-1/2				
V Coda, Ms. 74-1/2 to 79	74-1/2 to 76-1/2	Subject, dim.	T	normal	tonic (a)	g
	75-1/2 to 79	Answer, normal	S	inverted	dominant	g
	76-1/2 to 78-1/2	Subject, dim.'	A	normal	tonic	g

32

OVERALL STRUCTURE IN CONTRAPUNCTUS VII
(a4) Ms. 1-61

SECTION	MEASURE NOS.	FUGUE STATEMENT (with note values)	VOICE	ORDER	STARTING NOTE	KEY
I Exposition, Ms. 1 to 13-1/2	1-3	Subject, dim.	T	normal	tonic	d
	2-6	Answer, normal	S	inverted	dominant	d
	3-5	Subject, dim.	A	inverted	tonic (ends with c-sharp)	d
	5 to 13-1/2	Answer, augmented	B	inverted	tonic (ends with c-natural)	d
II Ms. 13-1/2 to 20	7-9	Subject, dim.	A	normal	tonic	a
	9-11	Answer, dim.	T	inverted	dominant	d
	13-1/2 to 15-1/2	Subject, dim.	S	normal, altered	tonic (a)	g
	14-1/2 to 18	Answer, normal	A	inverted, altered	dominant	g
	17-19	Subject, dim.	T	normal	tonic	B-flat Major

Episode (1)
Ms. 19-20

33

OVERALL STRUCTURE IN CONTRAPUNCTUS VII (continued)

SECTION	MEASURE NOS.	FUGUE STATEMENT (with note values)	VOICE	ORDER	STARTING NOTE	KEY
III Ms. 20-35	20-22	Subject, dim.	T	normal	tonic (c)	B-flat Major
	20-1/2 to 22 (23)	Answer, dim.	B	inverted, altered	dominant	B-flat Major
	23-25	Subject, dim.	A	normal	tonic	F
	23-1/2 to 31	Subject, augmented	T	normal, altered	tonic	F
	24-1/2 to 26-1/2	Answer, dim.	S	inverted	dominant	F
	24-1/2 to 31	(Tenor Subject continues)				
	28-30	Subject, dim.	B	normal	tonic	d
	29-1/2 to 31-1/2	Subject, dim.	A	normal	tonic	d
		Episode (2) Ms. 31-1/2 to 35				
IV Ms. 35-45	35-43	Answer, augmented	A	inverted	dominant	d
	36-1/2 to 40-1/2	Subject, normal	T	normal, altered	tonic	d
	38-1/4 to 42	Subject, normal	S	normal	tonic	d

34

OVERALL STRUCTURE IN CONTRAPUNCTUS VII (continued)

SECTION	MEASURE NOS.	FUGUE STATEMENT (with note values)	VOICE	ORDER	STARTING NOTE	KEY
(IV)	42-1/2 to 44-1/2	Answer, dim.	S	inverted	dominant	d
	43-45	Answer, dim.	A	inverted	dominant	d
V Ms. 45 to 49-3/4	45-47	Subject, dim.	A	normal	tonic (a)	g
	46-1/4 to 48-1/4	Answer, dim.	T	inverted	dominant	g
	47-3/4 to 49-3/4	Subject, dim.	B	normal	tonic (g)	F
	Episode (3) Ms. 49-3/4, one beat					
VI Ms. 50-61	50-58	Subject, augmented	S	normal	tonic	d
	51-53	Subject, dim.	A	inverted, altered	tonic (e)	d
	54-3/4 to 56-3/4	Subject, dim.	A	normal	tonic (e)	d
	55-57	Subject, dim.	T	normal	tonic (a)	g, modified
	Episode (4) (4-A) Ms. 58-60 (4-B) Ms. 60-61, CODA					

OVERALL STRUCTURE IN CONTRAPUNCTUS VIII
(a3) Ms. 1-168

SECTION	MEASURE NOS.	FUGUE STATEMENT	VOICE	ORDER	STARTING NOTE	KEY
DIVISION ONE Ms. 1 to 39-1/2						
I Exposition I, Ms. 1-17	1(1/2) to 5	Subject I	A	normal	tonic	d
		Episode (1) Ms. 5 to 6-1/2				
	6-1/2 to 10	Answer I	B	normal	dominant	d
		Episode (2) Ms. 10 to 11-1/2				
	11-1/2 to 15	Subject I	S	normal	tonic	d
		Episode (3) Ms. 15 to 21-1/2				
II Ms. 21-1/2 to 39-1/2	21-1/2 to 25	Answer I	A	normal	dominant	d
		Episode (4) Ms. 25 to 35-1/2				
	35-1/2 to 39-1/2	Subject I	B	normal	tonic	d
DIVISION TWO Ms. 39-1/2 to 93-1/2						
III Exposition II, M. 39-3/4 to 42 Ms. 39-1/2	39-1/2 to 43(1/2), M. 39-3/4 to 42	Subject I Subject II	S A	normal normal	tonic 6-flat	d d

36

OVERALL STRUCTURE IN CONTRAPUNCTUS VIII (continued)

SECTION	MEASURE NOS.	FUGUE STATEMENT	VOICE	ORDER	STARTING NOTE	KEY
(III)	43-1/2 to 47-1/2	Subject I	B	normal	tonic	g
	43-3/4 to 46	Answer II	S	normal	6-flat	g
		Episode (5) Ms. 47-1/2 to 49-1/2				
	49-1/2 to 53(1/2)	Answer I	A	normal	dominant	d
	49-3/4 to 52	Subject II	B	normal	6-natural	a
		Episode (6-A). Ms. 53-54 End of Exposition II Episode (6-B), Ms. 54 to 61-1/2				
$\underline{IV}$ Ms. 61-1/2 to 93-1/2						
$\underline{IVA}$ Ms. 61-1/2 to 67-3/4	61-1/2 to 65	Subject I	S	normal	tonic	F
	61-3/4 to 64	Subject II	A	normal	6-natural	F
		Episode (7) Ms. 65 to 67-3/4				
$\underline{IVB}$ Ms. 67-3/4 to 81-3/4	67-3/4 to 71	Subject I	B	normal	tonic	B-flat
	67-3/4 to 70	Subject II	S	normal	6-natural	Major
		Episode (8) Ms. 71 to 81-3/4				
$\underline{IVC}$ Ms. 81-3/4 to 93-1/2	81-3/4 to 85	Subject I	S	normal	tonic	d
	81-3/4 to 84	Subject II	A	normal	6-natural	d

37

OVERALL STRUCTURE IN CONTRAPUNCTUS VIII (continued)

SECTION	MEASURE NOS.	FUGUE STATEMENT	VOICE	ORDER	STARTING NOTE	KEY
		Episode (9-A), Ms. 85 to 93-1/2 End of Division Two Episode (9-B), Ms. 93-1/2 to 94-1/4				
DIVISION THREE (93-1/2) 94-1/4 to 124						
V Exposition III, Ms. 94-1/4 to 117-1/4	94-1/4 to 98	Subject III	A	inverted	dominant	d
		Episode (10) Ms. 98 to 99-1/4				
	99-1/4 to 103	Answer III	B	inverted	tonic	d
		Episode (11) Ms. 103 to 105-1/4				
	105-1/4 to 109	Subject III	S	inverted	dominant	a
		Episode (12-A), Ms. 109 to 117-1/4 End of Exposition III Episode (12-B), Ms. 117-1/4 to 124-1/2 Codetta for Division Three Episode (12-C), Ms. 124-1/2 to 125-1/2				
VIA Ms. (124-1/2) 125-1/2 to 131-1/2	125-1/2 to 129 125-1/4 to 127	Subject I Subject II	A S	normal normal	tonic dominant, abbreviated	d d

OVERALL STRUCTURE IN CONTRAPUNCTUS VIII (continued)

SECTION	MEASURE NOS.	FUGUE STATEMENT	VOICE	ORDER	STARTING NOTE	KEY
		Episode (13) Ms. 129 to 131-1/2				
VIB Ms. 131-1/2 to 147-1/2	131-1/2 to 135	Answer I	B	normal	dominant	d
	131-3/4 to 134	Subject II	A	normal	6-natural	a
		Episode (14) Ms. 135 to 147-1/2 (148)				
VIIA Ms. 147-1/2 to 152-1/2	147-1/2 to 151	Subject I	S	normal	tonic	F
	147-3/4 to 150	Subject II	A	normal	6-natural	F
	148-1/4 to 152	Subject III	B	inverted	dominant	F, altered
		Episode (15) Ms. 152 to 152-1/2				
VIIB Ms. 152-1/2 to 158-3/4	152-1/2 to 156	Answer I	A	normal	dominant	F
	152-3/4 to 155	Answer II	B	normal	3rd (6th)	F (C)
	153-1/4 to 157	Answer III	S	inverted	(tonic)	g, modulates
		Episode (16) Ms. 156 to 158-3/4				
VIIC Ms. 158-3/4 to 170-1/2	158-3/4 to 162	Subject I	B	normal	tonic	g
	158-3/4 to 161	Subject II	S	normal	6-flat	g
	159-1/4 to 163	Subject III	A	inverted	dominant	g

39

OVERALL STRUCTURE IN CONTRAPUNCTUS VIII (continued)

SECTION	MEASURE NOS.	FUGUE STATEMENT	VOICE	ORDER	STARTING NOTE	KEY
		Episode (17) Ms. 163 to 170-1/2				
VIID Ms. 170-1/2 to 180	170-1/2 to 174 170-3/4 to 173 171-1/4 to 175	Subject I Subject II Subject III	B A S	normal normal inverted	tonic 6-flat dominant	d d d
		Episode (18-A), Ms. 175-180				
		Episode (18-B), Ms. 180-182 Begins Coda				
VIII Coda, Ms. 180-188	182-3/4 to 186 182-3/4 to 185 183-1/4 to 187	Subject I Subject II Subject III	S A B	normal normal inverted	tonic 6-flat dominant	d d d
		Episode (19) Ms. 187-188				

OVERALL STRUCTURE IN CONTRAPUNCTUS IX
(a4) Ms. 1-130

SECTION	MEASURE NOS.	FUGUE STATEMENT	VOICE	ORDER	STARTING NOTE	KEY
$\underline{I}$ Ms. 1-35						
Exposition, Ms. 1-29	1(1/4) to 8	Subject I	A	normal	tonic	d
	8-1/4 to 15	Answer I	S	normal	dominant	d
	15-1/4 to 22	Subject I	B	normal	tonic	d
	22-1/4 to 29	Answer I	T	normal	dominant	d
		Episode (1) Ms. 29-35				
$\underline{II}$ Ms. 35-99						
$\underline{IIA}$ Ms. 35-45	35-43	Subject II (original Subject of this study, augmented)	S	normal	tonic	d
	35-1/4 to 42	Subject I	T	normal	tonic	d
		Episode (2) Ms. 43-45				
$\underline{IIB}$ Ms. 45-59	45-53	Answer II	T	normal	tonic	F
	45-1/4 to 52	Answer I	A	normal	dominant	F
		Episode (3) Ms. 53-59				

41

OVERALL STRUCTURE IN CONTRAPUNCTUS IX (continued)

SECTION	MEASURE NOS.	FUGUE STATEMENT	VOICE	ORDER	STARTING NOTE	KEY
IIC Ms. 59-73	59-67 59-1/4 to 66	Subject II Subject I	A B	normal normal	tonic tonic	d d
		Episode (4) Ms. 67-73				
IID Ms. 73-89	73-81 73-1/4 to 80	Answer II Answer I	T A	normal normal	tonic dominant	a a
		Episode (5) Ms. 81-89				
IIE Ms. 89-99	89-97 89-1/4 to 96	Subject II Answer I	B S	normal normal	tonic dominant	d d
		Episode (6) Ms. 97-99				
III Ms. 99-119	99-107 99-1/4 to 106	Subject II Answer I	T A	normal normal	tonic dominant	g g
		Episode (7) Ms. 107-119				
IV Coda, Ms. 119-130						
IVA Ms. 119-127	119-127 119-1/4 to 126	Subject II Subject I	A T	normal normal	tonic tonic	d d

42

OVERALL STRUCTURE IN CONTRAPUNCTUS IX (continued)

SECTION	MEASURE NOS.	FUGUE STATEMENT	VOICE	ORDER	STARTING NOTE	KEY
IVB Ms. 127-130		Episode (8) Ms. 127-130				

43

OVERALL STRUCTURE IN CONTRAPUNCTUS X
(a4) Ms. 1-120

SECTION	MEASURE NOS.	FUGUE STATEMENT	VOICE	ORDER	STARTING NOTE	KEY
DIVISION ONE Ms. 1(1/4) to 14-1/4						
I Exposition I, Ms. 1-1/4 to 12	1(1/4) to 4-1/2	Subject I	A	normal	7-sharp	d
	3-3/4 to 7	Answer I	T	normal	7-sharp	g
	7-1/4 to 10-1/2	Subject I	B	inverted	3-natural	d
	8-3/4 to 12	Answer I	S	inverted	3-natural	a, modulates
	Episode (1) Ms. 12 to 14-1/4					
II Ms. 14-1/4 to 23	14-1/4 to 17-1/2	Subject I	A	normal	modulates	(g)
	14-3/4 to 18	Answer I	T	inverted	modulates	(g)
	Episode (2) Ms. 18-23					
DIVISION TWO Ms. 23-44						
III Exposition II, Ms. 23-38	23-27	Subject II	S	inverted	dominant	d
	(24-26 false entry, Answer incomplete	Answer II	A	inverted	tonic	d)

44

OVERALL STRUCTURE IN CONTRAPUNCTUS X (continued)

SECTION	MEASURE NOS.	FUGUE STATEMENT	VOICE	ORDER	STARTING NOTE	KEY
(III)	26-30	Answer II	T	inverted	tonic	d
		Episode (3) M. 30				
	31-35	Subject II	B	inverted	dominant	d
	34-38	Answer II	A	inverted	tonic	d
		Episode (4-A) Ms. 38-42, completion of Division Two				
		Episode (4-B) Ms. 42-44				
IVA Ms. 44-52	44-48	Subject II	A	inverted	dominant	d
	44-1/4 to 47-1/2	Answer I	T	normal	7-sharp	g
		Episode (5) Ms. 47-1/2 to 52				
IVB Ms. 52-66	52-56	Answer II	B	inverted	tonic	d, modulates
	52-1/4 to 55-1/2	Answer I	A	normal	4th (5th)	a, modulates
		Episode (6) Ms. 56-66				
IVC Ms. 66-75	66-70	Subject II	T	inverted	dominant	d
	66-1/4 to 69-1/2	Subject I	S	normal	dominant	d

OVERALL STRUCTURE IN CONTRAPUNCTUS X (continued)

SECTION	MEASURE NOS.	FUGUE STATEMENT	VOICE	ORDER	STARTING NOTE	KEY
		Episode (7) Ms. 70-75				
VA Ms. 75-85	75-79	Subject II	S	inverted	dominant	d
	75-79	Subject II	A	inverted	dominant	F
	75-1/4 to 78-1/2	Subject I	B	normal	dominant	(d)
		Episode (8) Ms. 79-85				
VB Ms. 85-103	85-89	Subject II	B	inverted	dominant (g)	d
	85-1/4 to 88-1/2	Subject I	S	normal	7-sharp	d
	85-1/4 to 88-1/2	Subject I	A	normal	4th (5th)	d
		Episode (9) Ms. 89-103				
VC Ms. 103(1/4) to 115	103(1/4) to 107	Subject II	S	inverted	(tonic)	F, modulates
	103-1/4 to 106-1/2	Answer I	T	normal	7-natural	g
	103-1/4 to 106-1/2	Answer I	B	normal	dominant	g
		Episode (10) Ms. 107-115				
VD Coda, Ms. 115-120	115-119	Subject II	B	inverted	dominant	d
	115-1/4 to 118-1/2	Subject I	A	normal	7-sharp	d
	115-1/4 to 118-1/2	Subject I	T	normal	dominant	d
		Episode (11) Ms. 119-120				

SECTION	MEASURE NOS.	FUGUE STATEMENT	VOICE	ORDER	STARTING NOTE	KEY
DIVISION ONE Ms. 1 to 27-1/2						
I Exposition I, Ms. 1-18	(1)1/4 to 5	Subject I (inversion of Subject III in Contrapunctus VIII)	A	normal	tonic	d
	5-1/4 to 9	Answer I	S	normal	dominant	d
	9-1/4 to 13	Subject I	B	normal	tonic	d
	13-1/4 to 17	Answer I	T	normal	dominant	d
		Episode (1-A), Ms. 17 to 18-1/2 End of Exposition I				
		Episode (1-B), Ms. 18-1/4 to 22				
II Ms. 22-1/4 to 27-1/2	22-1/4 to 26	Subject I	S	normal	tonic (e)	d
		Episode (2) Ms. 26 to 27-1/2				
DIVISION TWO Ms. 27-1/2 to 71						
III Exposition II, Ms. 27-1/2 to 60	27-1/2 to 34-1/2	Subject II (inversion of Subject I in Triple Fugue Contrapunctus VIII)	A	inverted	dominant	d
		Episode (3) Ms. 31 to 34-1/2				
	34-1/2 to 44	Answer II	T	inverted	dominant	a

47

OVERALL STRUCTURE IN CONTRAPUNCTUS XI (continued)

SECTION	MEASURE NOS.	FUGUE STATEMENT	VOICE	ORDER	STARTING NOTE	KEY
(III)		Episode (4) Ms. 38-44				
	43-3/4 to 47	Subject II	B	inverted	dominant	d
		Episode (5) Ms. 47-57				
	57-60	Answer II (based on original Subject I, M. 1, in Contrapunctus VIII)	S	normal	tonic	d
		Episode (6-A), Ms. 60 to 61-1/4 End of Exposition II Episode (6-B), Ms. 61-1/4 to 67-3/4				
IV Ms. 67-3/4 to 71	67-3/4 to 71	Answer II	B	normal	tonic	a
DIVISION THREE Ms. 71-1/4 to 89-1/2						
V Exposition I-A, Ms. 71-1/4 to 89-1/2	71-1/4 to 75	Answer I	T	inverted	dominant	a
		Episode (7) Ms. 75 to 76-1/4				
	76-1/4 to 80	Answer I	S	inverted	dominant	d
	80-1/4 to 84	Subject I	B	inverted	tonic	d

48

OVERALL STRUCTURE IN CONTRAPUNCTUS XI (continued)

SECTION	MEASURE NOS.	FUGUE STATEMENT	VOICE	ORDER	STARTING NOTE	KEY
	84-1/4 to 88	Answer I	A	inverted	dominant	d
	(Previous four statements in Exposition I-A now similar to Subject III and Answer III of Contrapunctus VIII, in reverse order.)					
		Episode (8) Ms. 88 to 89-1/2, end of Division III				
DIVISION FOUR Ms. 89-1/2 to 117						
VI Exposition III, Ms. 89-1/2 to 109						
VIA Ms. 89-1/2 to 93-3/4	89-1/2 to 93	Subject II	B	inverted	dominant	d
	89-3/4 to 92-1/2	Subject III (retrograde version of Subject II in Contrapunctus VIII, extended by two beats)	T	retrograde	2-flat	
	90-3/4 to 93	Subject III, modified	A	retrograde	6-flat	d
		Episode (9) Ms. 93-1/4 to 93-3/4, 2 beats				
VIB Ms. 93-3/4 to 100	93-3/4 to 97	Answer II	A	inverted	dominant	a
	93-3/4 to 96-1/2	Answer III	S	retrograde	2-flat	a
		Episode (10) Ms. 97-100				

49

OVERALL STRUCTURE IN CONTRAPUNCTUS XI (continued)

SECTION	MEASURE NOS.	FUGUE STATEMENT	VOICE	ORDER	STARTING NOTE	KEY
VIC Ms. 100-1/4 to 105	100-1/4 to 102-1/2	Subject III, modified at end	B	normal	dominant	d
	101-1/4 to 105	Subject I	A	normal	tonic	d
VID Ms. 105-1/4 to 111-3/4	105-1/4 to 107-1/2	Answer III, modified at end	A	normal	dominant	d
	105-1/2 to 109	Subject II	T	normal	tonic	d
	Episode (11) Ms. 109 to 111-3/4					
Intermediate Section (A), 111-3/4 to 114 Ms. 111-3/4 to 114		Subject III (false entry)	B	normal	6-natural	B-flat Major
VIE Ms. 113-3/4 to 117	113-3/4 to 117	Subject II	S	inverted	dominant	d
	113-3/4 to 116-1/2	Subject III	A	retrograde	2-flat	d
VII Ms. 117-1/4 to 130						
VIIA 117-1/4 to 120-1/2	117-1/4 to 120	Subject III	S	normal	4-natural	d, modulates
	117-3/4 to 120-1/2	Subject III	A	normal	tonic	d, modulates

50

OVERALL STRUCTURE IN CONTRAPUNCTUS XI (continued)

SECTION	MEASURE NOS.	FUGUE STATEMENT	VOICE	ORDER	STARTING NOTE	KEY
VIIB Ms. 120-1/2 to 125	120-1/2 to 124-1/2	Subject III, extended	A	retrograde	3-sharp	d, modulates
	122-1/4 to 124-1/2	Subject III	S	retrograde	tonic	d, modulates
	Episode (12) Ms. 124-1/2 to 125					
VIIC Ms. 125 to 130	125 to 127-1/2	Subject III	T	normal	dominant	d
	125-1/2 to 128	Subject III, abbreviated	B	normal	tonic	d
	Episode (13) Ms. 128-130					
Intermediate Section (B) Ms. 130-1/4 to 132-1/2	130-1/4	Subject III, abbreviated	B	normal	dominant	d
	130-3/4 to 132-1/2	Subject III, abbreviated	S	inverted	7-sharp	d
	130-3/4 to 132	Subject III	A	inverted	2-natural	d
	130-3/4 to 132-1/4	Subject III	T	normal	6-flat	d
VIII Ms. 132-1/4 to 136-3/4	132-1/4 to 136	Subject I	B	normal	tonic	d
	Episode (14) Ms. 136 to 136-3/4					
IX Ms. 136-3/4 to 140	136-3/4 to 140	Subject II	T	inverted	dominant	d
	136-3/4 to 139-1/2	Subject III	A	retrograde	2-flat	d
	137-1/4 to 140	Subject III modified	S	retrograde	dominant	d

51

214256

OVERALL STRUCTURE IN CONTRAPUNCTUS XI (continued)

SECTION	MEASURE NOS.	FUGUE STATEMENT	VOICE	ORDER	STARTING NOTE	KEY
Intermediate Section (C), Ms. 140-1/4 to 146	140-1/4 to 141-1/2	Subject III (false entry)	T	normal	dominant	d
	141-1/4 to 143-1/2	Subject III	B	inverted	tonic	d
	142-1/4 to 144	Subject III, abbreviated	S	normal	dominant	d
	142-1/2 to 144	Subject III	A	normal	2-flat	d
		Episode (15) Ms. 144-146				
X Ms. 145-3/4 to 152-3/4	145-3/4 to 149	Subject II	S	inverted	dominant	e
	145-3/4 to 148-1/2	Subject III	A	retrograde	2-natural	e
	146-1/4 to 150	Subject I	T	normal	tonic	e
		Episode (16) Ms. 150-1/4 to 152-3/4				
XI Ms. 152-3/4 to 175						
XIA Ms. 152-3/4 to 158	152-3/4 to 155	Subject III	S	inverted	tonic	d
	152-3/4 to 154-1/2	Subject III (mirror statement)	A	normal	dominant	d
		Episode (17) Ms. 155 to 158				
XIB Ms. 158-1/4 to 164-1/4	158-1/4 to 162	Answer I	S	inverted	dominant	d
	158-1/4 to 162	Subject I (mirror statement)	A	normal	tonic (e)	d

SECTION	MEASURE NOS.	FUGUE STATEMENT	VOICE	ORDER	STARTING NOTE	KEY
		Episode (18) Ms. 162-1/4 to 164-1/4				
XIC 164-1/4 to 168 Ms. 164-1/4 to 168	164-1/4 to 168	Subject I	T	normal	tonic	g
		Answer I (mirror statement)	B	inverted	dominant	g
Intermediate Section (D),	167-3/4 to 171	Subject III	S	inverted	3-natural	d
	168-1/4 to 169-1/2	Subject III	A	retrograde inversion	3-natural	d, modulates
Ms. 167-3/4 to 175	169-1/4 to 171	Subject III, abbreviated	T	inverted	tonic	d
	169-3/4 to 172-1/2	Subject III	B	normal	6-flat	d
		Episode (19) Ms. 172-1/2 to 175				
XII Coda, Ms. 174-3/4 to 184						
XIIA Ms. 174-3/4 to 179	174-3/4 to 178	Subject II	B	inverted	dominant	d
	175-1/4 to 177	Subject III	T	retrograde	3-natural	d
	175-1/4 to 179	Subject I	A	normal	tonic	d
		Episode (20) Ms. 179 to 179-3/4				
XIIB Ms. 179-3/4 to 184	179-3/4 to 182	Subject III	B	retrograde	2-flat	d
	179-3/4 to 183	Subject II	T	inverted	dominant	d
	180-1/4 to 184	Subject I	S	normal	tonic	d

53

OVERALL STRUCTURE IN CONTRAPUNCTUS XVI – RECTUS
(a3) Ms. 1-71

SECTION	MEASURE NOS.	FUGUE STATEMENT	VOICE	ORDER	STARTING NOTE	KEY
I Ms. 1-20 Exposition, Ms. 1-13	1-5	Subject	A	inverted	dominant	d
	5-9	Answer	B	normal	tonic	d
	9-13	Subject	S	inverted	tonic	d
		Episode (1) Ms. 13-20				
II 20-29	20-24	Answer	A	normal	tonic	d
		Episode (2) Ms. 24-29				
III Ms. 29-48	29-33	Subject	B	inverted	dominant	B-flat Major
	33-37	Answer	S	normal	tonic	B-flat Major
	37-41	Subject	A	inverted	dominant	g
		Episode (3) Ms. 41-48				
IV Ms. 48-62	48-52	Answer	A	normal	tonic (e)	d
		Episode (4) Ms. 52-62				

54

OVERALL STRUCTURE IN CONTRAPUNCTUS XVI – RECTUS (continued)

SECTION	MEASURE NOS.	FUGUE STATEMENT	VOICE	ORDER	STARTING NOTE	KEY
V Coda, Ms. 62-71	62-66	Subject	B	inverted	dominant (g)	d
	66-70	Answer	S	normal	tonic	d
		Episode (5) Ms. 70-71				

55

OVERALL STRUCTURE IN CONTRAPUNCTUS XVI – INVERSUS
(a3) Ms. 1-71

SECTION	MEASURE NOS.	FUGUE STATEMENT	VOICE	ORDER	STARTING NOTE	KEY
I Ms. 1-20 Exposition, Ms. 1-13	1-5	Subject	S	normal	tonic	d
	5-9	Answer	A	inverted	dominant	d
	9-13	Subject	B	normal	dominant	d, modulates
		Episode (1) Ms. 13-20				
II Ms. 20-29	20-24	Answer	S	inverted	dominant	d
		Episode (2) Ms. 24-29				
III Ms. 29-48	29-33	Subject	A	normal	tonic	F
	33-37	Answer	B	inverted	dominant	F
	37-41	Subject	S	normal	tonic	a
		Episode (3) Ms. 41-48				
IV Ms. 48-62	48-52	Answer	S	inverted	dominant (g)	d
		Episode (4) Ms. 52-62				

56

OVERALL STRUCTURE IN CONTRAPUNCTUS XVI - INVERSUS (continued)

SECTION	MEASURE NOS.	FUGUE STATEMENT	VOICE	ORDER	STARTING NOTE	KEY
$\frac{V}{\text{Coda}}$, Ms. 62-71	62-66	Subject	A	normal	tonic (e)	d
	66-70	Answer	B	inverted	dominant	d
		Episode (5) Ms. 70-71				

OVERALL STRUCTURE IN CONTRAPUNCTUS XVII – RECTUS
(a4) Ms. 1-56

SECTION	MEASURE NOS.	FUGUE STATEMENT	VOICE	ORDER	STARTING NOTE	KEY
I Exposition, Ms. 1-21	1-5	Subject	B	normal	tonic	d
	5-9	Answer	T	normal	dominant	d
		Episode (1) Ms. 9-1/4 to 10, 3 beats				
	10-14	Subject	A	normal	tonic	d
	14-18	Answer	S	normal	dominant	d
		Episode (2) Ms. 18-21				
II Ms. 21-50	21-25	Subject	S	normal	tonic	d
		Episode (3) Ms. 25-1/4 to 26				
	26-30	Subject	A	normal	tonic	g
		Episode (4) Ms. 30-32				
	32-36	Subject	T	normal	tonic	B-flat Major
		Episode (5) Ms. 36-42				

58

OVERALL STRUCTURE IN CONTRAPUNCTUS XVII – RECTUS (continued)

SECTION	MEASURE NOS.	FUGUE STATEMENT	VOICE	ORDER	STARTING NOTE	KEY
(II)	42-46	Subject	B	normal	tonic	d

(All the Subjects stated in Section II are elaborated versions of the basic Subject of this mirror fugue.)

Episode (6)
Ms. 46-50

| III Ms. 50-56 | 50-54 | Subject | A | normal | tonic | d |

(Still additional elaboration is given to this last statement of the Subject.)

Episode (7) CODA
Ms. 54-56

OVERALL STRUCTURE IN CONTRAPUNCTUS XVII – INVERSUS
(a4) Ms. 1-56

SECTION	MEASURE NOS.	FUGUE STATEMENT	VOICE	ORDER	STARTING NOTE	KEY
I Exposition, Ms. 1-21	1-5	Subject	S	inverted	dominant	d
	5-9	Answer	A	inverted	tonic	d
		Episode (1) Ms. 9-1/4 to 10, 3 beats				
	10-14	Subject	T	inverted	dominant	d
	14-18	Answer	B	inverted	tonic	d
		Episode (2) Ms. 18-21				
II Ms. 21-50	21-25	Subject	B	inverted	dominant	d
		Episode (3) Ms. 25-1/4 to 26				
	26-30	Subject	T	inverted	dominant	a
		Episode (4) Ms. 30-32				
	32-36	Subject	A	inverted	dominant	F
		Episode (5) Ms. 36-42				

60

OVERALL STRUCTURE IN CONTRAPUNCTUS XVII – INVERSUS (continued)

SECTION	MEASURE NOS.	FUGUE STATEMENT	VOICE	ORDER	STARTING NOTE	KEY
(II)	42-46	Subject	S	inverted	dominant	d

(All the Subjects stated in Section II are elaborated versions of the basic subject of this mirror fugue.)

Episode (6)
Ms. 46-50

SECTION	MEASURE NOS.	FUGUE STATEMENT	VOICE	ORDER	STARTING NOTE	KEY
III Ms. 50-56	50-54	Subject	T	inverted	dominant	d

(Additional elaboration is given to this last statement of the subject.)

Episode (7) CODA
Ms. 54-56

61

OVERALL STRUCTURE IN CONTRAPUNCTUS XVIII
(a4) Ms. 1-239

SECTION	MEASURE NOS.	FUGUE STATEMENT	VOICE	ORDER	STARTING NOTE	KEY
DIVISION ONE Ms. 1-115						
<u>I</u> Exposition I, Ms. 1 to 21-1/2	(1)1/2 to 6-1/2	Subject I	B	normal	tonic	d
	6-1/2 to 11-1/2	Answer I	T	normal	dominant	d
	11-1/2 to 16-1/2	Subject I	A	normal	tonic	d
	16-1/2 to 21-1/2	Answer I	S	normal	dominant	d
<u>II</u> Ms. 21-1/2 to 43-1/4						
<u>IIA</u> Ms. 21-1/2 to 30-1/2	21-1/2 to 26-1/2	Subject I	B	inverted	tonic	d
	24-1/2 to 29-1/2	Subject I	T	normal	tonic	d
		Episode (1) Ms. 29-1/2 to 30-1/2				
<u>IIB</u> Ms. 30-1/2 to 37-1/2	30-1/2 to 35-1/2	Answer I	A	inverted	dominant	d
		Episode (2) Ms. 35-1/2 to 37-1/2				
<u>IIC</u> 37-1/2 to	37-1/2 to 42-1/4	Answer I	S	normal	dominant	d
	38-1/2 to 43-1/4	Subject I	A	normal	tonic	d

62

OVERALL STRUCTURE IN CONTRAPUNCTUS XVIII (continued)

SECTION	MEASURE NOS.	FUGUE STATEMENT	VOICE	ORDER	STARTING NOTE	KEY
		Episode (3) Ms. 43-1/4 (one beat)				
$\frac{\text{III}}{\text{Ms. } 43\text{-}1/2 \text{ to } 61\text{-}1/2}$	43-1/2 to 48-1/2	Subject I	B	normal	tonic (g)	F
		Episode (4) Ms. 48-1/2 to 55-1/2				
	55-1/2 to 60-1/2	Answer I	T	inverted	dominant	g
		Episode (5) Ms. 60-1/2 to 61-1/2				
$\frac{\text{IV}}{\text{Ms. } 61\text{-}1/2 \text{ to } 81}$						
$\frac{\text{IVA}}{\text{Ms. } 61\text{-}1/2 \text{ to } 67\text{-}1/2}$	61-1/2 to 66-1/2	Subject I	B	normal	tonic	d
	62-1/2 to 67-1/2	Subject I	S	normal	tonic (a)	g
		Episode (6) Ms. 67-1/2 to 71				
$\frac{\text{IVB}}{\text{Ms. } 71 \text{ to } 77\text{-}1/2}$	71 to 76-1/2	Answer I	A	inverted	dominant	B-flat Major
	72-1/2 to 77-1/2	Answer I	T	inverted	dominant (g)	F Major
		Episode (7) Ms. 77-1/2 to 81-1/2				

OVERALL STRUCTURE IN CONTRAPUNCTUS XVIII (continued)

SECTION	MEASURE NOS.	FUGUE STATEMENT	VOICE	ORDER	STARTING NOTE	KEY
V Ms. 81-1/2 to 89-1/2	81-1/2 to 86-1/2	Subject I	A	normal	tonic	d
		Episode (8) Ms. 86-1/2 to 89-1/2				
VI Ms. 89-1/2 to 105-3/4	89-1/2 to 94-1/4	Subject I	B	normal	tonic	B-flat Major
	92-1/2 to 97-1/2	Subject I	A	normal	tonic	g
	97-1/2 to 102-1/4	Subject I	T	normal	tonic (a)	g, modulates
	99-1/2 to 104-1/4	Subject I	A	normal	tonic	d
		Episode (9) Ms. 104-1/4 to 105-3/4				
VII Ms. 105-3/4 to 115	105-3/4 to 110-1/2	Subject I	B	normal	tonic	d
		Episode (10) Ms. 110-1/2 to 115				

DIVISION TWO

Ms. 114-1/4 to 193-1/4

| VIII Exposition II, Ms. 114-1/4 to 147-1/4 | 114-1/4 to 121 | Subject II | A | normal | 3-natural | d |
| | 121-1/4 to 127 | Answer II | S | normal | 3-natural | a |

64

OVERALL STRUCTURE IN CONTRAPUNCTUS XVIII (continued)

SECTION	MEASURE NOS.	FUGUE STATEMENT	VOICE	ORDER	STARTING NOTE	KEY
(VIII)		Episode (11) Ms. 127-1/4 to 128-1/4				
	128-1/4 to 135	Subject II	B	normal	3-natural	d
	135-1/4 to 141	Answer II	T	normal	3-natural	a
		Episode (12) Ms. 141-1/4 to 147-1/4				
IX Ms. 147-1/4 to 180-1/4						
IXA Ms. 147-1/4 to 156-1/4	147-1/4 to 154 148-1/2 to 153-1/2	Subject II Subject I	S B	normal normal	3-natural tonic	d d
		Episode (13) Ms. 154-1/4 to 156-1/4				
IXB Ms. 156-1/4 to 167-1/4	156-1/4 to 162 157-1/2 to 162	Answer II Subject I (rhythmically altered)	A T	normal normal	3-natural tonic	a a
		Episode (14) Ms. 162-1/4 to 167-1/4				
IXC Ms. 167-1/4 to 180-1/4	167-1/4 to 173 169-1/2 to 174-1/2	Subject II Subject I	T S	normal normal	3-natural tonic	F F

65

OVERALL STRUCTURE IN CONTRAPUNCTUS XVIII (continued)

SECTION	MEASURE NOS.	FUGUE STATEMENT	VOICE	ORDER	STARTING NOTE	KEY
(IX)		Episode (15) Ms. 174-1/2 to 180-1/4				
X Ms. 180-1/4 to 193-1/4	180-1/4 to 186	Subject II	B	normal	3-flat	g
	182-1/2 to 187	Subject I (altered)	A	normal	tonic	g
	183-1/2 to 188-1/2	Subject I	S	normal	tonic (d)	c
		Episode (16) Ms. 188-1/2 to 193-1/4				

DIVISION THREE
Ms. 193-1/2 to 233

SECTION	MEASURE NOS.	FUGUE STATEMENT	VOICE	ORDER	STARTING NOTE	KEY
XI Ms. 193-1/2 to 210-1/2 Exposition III, Ms. 193-1/2 to 207-1/4	193-1/2 to 197-1/4	Subject III	T	normal	6-flat	d
	195-1/2 to 199	Answer III	A	normal	3-natural	d
		Episode (17) Ms. 199-1/4 to 201-1/2				
	201-1/2 to 205	Subject III	S	normal	6-flat	d
	203-1/2 to 207-1/4	Answer III	B	normal	3-natural	d(a)

Episode (18), Ms. 205-1/4 to 210-1/2
Episode (18-A), Ms. 205-1/4 to 207-1/4
End of Exposition III

66

OVERALL STRUCTURE IN CONTRAPUNCTUS XVIII (continued)

SECTION	MEASURE NOS.	FUGUE STATEMENT	VOICE	ORDER	STARTING NOTE	KEY
XII Ms. 210-1/2 to 222	210-1/2 to 214	Subject III	T	normal	6-flat	d
	213-1/2 to 216	Subject III	A	inverted	2-natural	d
		Episode (19) Ms. 216 to 217-1/2				
	217-1/2 to 221	Subject III	S	normal	6-flat	d
	218-222	Answer III	B	normal	3-natural	d (a)
XIII Ms. 222-1/2 to 233	222-1/2 to 225	Subject III	B	inverted	6-natural	c
	225-1/4 to 229	Answer III (rhythmically changed to enter on weak beat)	T	normal	2-flat	d
	226-1/2 to 230	Subject III	A	normal	6-flat	d
		Episode (20) Ms. 230 to 233				
XIV INCOMPLETE	233-1/4 to 239	Subject II	A	normal	2-natural	d
	234-1/2 to 239	Subject I	B	normal	tonic	d
	235-1/2 to 239	Subject III	T	normal	6-flat	d

67

BRIEF DESCRIPTIVE ANALYSES OF EACH OF THE FUGUES

THE FOUR SIMPLE FUGUES

Contrapunctus I: Contrapunctus I is divided into three sections. The original order of the entry of voices as stated in the exposition guides the entrances of voices in the next two sections. All statements of the subject and answer are presented in normal order. The answer is tonal.

Reference is made to the key of the subdominant or G Minor both near the end of the exposition and at the end of the coda.

The episodes incorporate strict imitation, primarily based on motives of the counter-subject as stated with the answer in Ms. 6 and 7. All but the last episode are written in three voices, the omitted voice preparing for the next entrance of either the subject or answer.

The coda presents the answer by the T, the same voice that completed the exposition. The fugue begins and ends with inner voices.

Contrapunctus II: Contrapunctus II is divided into five sections, with all statements of the subject and answer being stated in normal order. All sections present the subject and answer in D Minor, except Section III.

The subject is the same as the original subject of this study, except for the inclusion of a dotted rhythm with motive (3). This dotted rhythm permeates the entire fugue. While the element of rhythm is important in this fugue, only the one type of dotted rhythm having a dotted eighth and sixteenth notes is used, unlike Contrapunctus VI and Contrapunctus XIII and the Canon alla Decima.

The answer is tonal. The exposition begins and ends with the outer voices. Section II has all four voices presenting the subject and answer, but begins and ends with the inner voices. Section II has one stretto statement of the subject with the answer.

Section III presents three successive statements of the subject in different keys and expanded range in the outer voices. Section IV presents one final statement of the subject and answer, back in D Minor.

In Section IV, the answer appears with a syncopated entry on the weak beat, so that all notes for the first half of the answer appear on weak beats.

The subject is stated by the S in the coda in Section V, the same voice that concluded the exposition.

Contrapunctus III: Contrapunctus III has three levels of contrapuntal interest: a complete fugue based on the original subject of this study in inverted order, presented in Sections I, II, and III; intermediate sections based on a variant of the subject similar to the subject of the stretto fugues, in Intermediate Sections A and B; and the episodes.

The two intermediate sections offer contrast to the main fugue in several ways. The omission of the bass subject or answer gives to the intermediate sections a secondary interest. The first intermediate section is primarily in a three-voice structure, and its style can be compared to the Baroque trio sonata, with the upper two voices imitative and the lower voice having continuous movement like a basso continuo. The second intermediate section begins to lose its trio sonata implication when the fourth voice is added, although the upper two voices still seem complementary as paired voices in a trio sonata. The episodes are fundamentally imitative, take on the characteristics of the intermediate sections, and serve a transitional function, although the imitation becomes quite dense for emphasis.

The subject in Contrapunctus III becomes the main answer in Contrapunctus IV; the main answer in Contrapunctus III becomes the subject in Contrapunctus IV. The answer is emphasized in Contrapunctus III, whereas the subject is emphasized in Contrapunctus IV.

The entire Contrapunctus III is highly chromatic.

Section I includes the exposition, beginning with an inner voice and ending with an outer voice, with all statements of the main subject in inverted order. The second episode prepares the texture for the entrance of the varied statements of the subject. The answer of the fugue is tonal.

Intermediate Section A presents three statements of the variation of the answer in the S and T, gradually becoming lower in range. A trio sonata texture is retained. The voices all are syncopated statements.

Section II has two statements of the main answer more expanded in range than the exposition. Intermediate Section B presents two statements of the variant of the main answer, now starting on the main beats of the respective measures. Section III presents one final statement of the main answer and concludes with a brief coda.

An emphasis is shown to the answer in this fugue, since all statements of the subject following the exposition begin fundamentally on the dominant and could be said to be statements of the answer, in all sections.

Contrapunctus IV: At no time in this fugue does the subject of the stretto fugues appear, as was found in Contrapunctus III in the intermediate sections. The subject of this Contrapunctus IV is the same as the answer in Contrapunctus III; the Answer is the same as the subject in Contrapunctus III.

Five major sections exist, with emphasis on the subject, throughout this fugue. The order of entries of the voices as stated in the exposition serves as the basis for the subsequent entries, as follows:

Exposition	S A T B
Section II	S A T B
Section III	B T A S (reverse order)
Section IV	T B A S
Section V	T A

The exposition begins and ends with outer voices; the coda (Section V) with inner voices. Section IV retains the same paired voices, but reverses B and T. Sections I and III have episodes between the second and third statements. Sections II and IV have no episodes between the entrances of the statements.

Sections II and III present the subject in various keys, the modulations of the subject occurring in cycles of fifths:

70

Section II: F C g d

Section III: C g d a

Section IV shows a fifth relationship:

Ms. 107-111   d B-flat)
Ms. 111-115   d F   ) Interval of a 5th

Section V progresses from G Minor to D Minor.

In Section IV the tight stretto after one beat for the subject and answer serves as a climax to the four simple fugues; illustrates another possible combination of the subject; and might be said to anticipate the next group of stretto fugues.

The material other than the subject, answer, and counter-subject is vital to the procedure of this fugue. The close association of the lengthy episodes and the free material creates an even balance with the rest of the fugue structure. The constant usage of paired voices in varying imitative combinations serves to strategically anticipate the climactic paired stretto subjects and answers in Section IV.

As an interesting detail of style, the skip of a descending third, called a "cuckoo" motive by Tovey, is emphasized in both the episodes and the free material.

The rests that occur in this fugue exist to prepare the entrance of a new statement of subject or answer, or to lighten the texture by including numerous rests between small motives. These usages of rests can be seen in the following measures:

Ms. 19-23	Tenor	Rests between short motives to lighten texture of episode
Ms. 23-26	Soprano	Complete measure rests to prepare for entrance of S subject in M. 27
Ms. 35-38	Bass	Complete measure rests to prepare for entrance of B subject

71

Ms. 43-46	Alto and	Rests between short
	Bass	motives to lighten
		texture of episode

Similar analyses can be made throughout the fugue. Complete measure rests to prepare for a new statement of the subject are not reserved for the episode sections. Rather, the two longest episodes retain a basic four-part structure. The tightness of the imitative sections in the episodes lightens the texture or strengthens the texture. From M. 81 to the end of the fugue, a basic four-part structure is found. The two stretto statements plus the coda do not have lengthy measures of rests to introduce any one subject. The texture is varied to produce gradations of dynamic intensity.

As an incidental observation, a recurring cadential figure is found in the following passages:

Ms. 51-52	Tenor
Ms. 101-102	Tenor
Ms. 114-115	Bass, serving as the figure for imitation in the first part of Episode (6)
M. 123	Alto
M. 129	Soprano, overlapping with the beginning of the coda

THE THREE STRETTO FUGUES

Contrapunctus V: The subject of the three stretto fugues expands upon the original subject of this study by added passing-notes and changes in rhythm. This subject appears in the two intermediate sections of Contrapunctus III, somewhat modified. All the stretto fugues are in C meter, rather than ₵, as found in the four simple fugues.

The presentation of the first four voices in each exposition of the three stretto fugues combines the types of note values heard in the respective fugue. The exposition creates the setting for the procedures to follow. The stretto entrances become tighter with each successive fugue.

The six sections of Contrapunctus V vary the entrances of the second stretto voice. The first statement of the subject in all three stretto fugues is answered in contrary motion.

In Sections I and II all voices enter after three measures, with no intervening episodes. Section II varies from the first section in having one statement in A Minor and in a varying order of voices. In Section III the second voice enters after one-half measure, or two beats, the first two statements being in F Major, the second two in G Minor. Episodes separate and complete the successive two statements. In Section IV the second voice enters after one and one-half measures, the first two statements being in B-flat Major, the second two in D Minor, with episodes between two statements. Section V presents the second voice after one measure, all voices being stated in D Minor. In Sections IV and V, the subject is stated in stretto with itself, as is the answer. The last statement of the subject occurs in the coda in mirror stretto with the answer.

Throughout the fugue, the subject is heard in stretto with itself, and in stretto with the answer, in various combinations and in invertible counterpoint, as is the answer combined with itself and the subject.

The order of subject and answer in the exposition is planned to permit the mirror combination in the coda. The same two voices end the fugue as began the exposition, although the parts are reversed.

Because of the entrance of the voices after three measures in the first two secions, a double exposition seems a possible analysis.

Section V, or the last group of four voices, is altered, as frequently is done in the simple fugues. Here the T is repeated twice and the B is omitted. In all other groupings of voices before the coda, all four voices are present.

In the exposition, both subject and answer are presented in normal and inverted orders. After the exposition, the subject is always stated inverted, beginning and ending on the dominant, while the answer is stated in normal order, beginning and ending on the tonic. The normal statement of the subject is differentiated from the normal statement of the answer by the ending of the subject on the supertonic. Numerous distinct sections occur throughout the fugue. Two intermediate episodes exist in the basically cadential episodes, as is explained under "Episodes". The answer is tonal.

The exposition begins and ends with inner voices. The coda ends with the A and Bass I. The disguised nature of the entrance of the A is in keeping with the many unexpected entrances of the subject or answer in this fugue. The disguised entrance of the A further serves to alleviate too blatant a beginning for the stretto presentation of the answer with the B subject i mirror imitation.

The sections in Contrapunctus V give evidence of Bach's consideration of the expansion and contraction o the voices presenting the subject or answer. Section I begins and ends with inner voices; Section II begins with an outer voice and ends with an inner voice; Section III has the two outer voices answered by the two inner voices; Section IV has the two lower voices answered by the two upper voices; Sections V and VI show the subject gradually progressing from a higher to a lower voice.

Contrapunctus VI: Contrapunctus VI states the subject and answer in normal note values and in diminution All statements of the subject are in normal order, beginning and ending on the tonic. All statements of the answer are in inverted order, beginning and ending on the dominant.

This fugue seems best analyzed by dividing the entire fugue into two major divisions. The first division emphasizes the subject with normal note values in stretto combinations with itself and the answer in diminution. Division Two emphasizes the answer in normal note values, combined in stretto with itself and th subject, again in diminution. A pivot section exists toward the end of Division One to change the emphasis from the subject of the first division to the answer in the second division.

An analysis of the five sections in each of the two divisions follows:

DIVISION ONE
Ms. 1-35

Section I. The subject is first stated in the exposition in normal values, with the remaining three statements in diminution, all in D Minor. A three-voice stretto results from the first three entries.

Section II. The subject in normal note values is combined below the subject in diminution. The subject

74

n diminution enters after 2-1/2 measures. Both state-
ents are in A Minor.

Section III. The subject in normal note values is
ombined in stretto with two statements of the answer
n diminution, all statements remaining in D Minor.

Section IV. This section serves as a pivot sec-
ion to permit the shift in emphasis from the subject
o the answer. The answer is first stated by itself
ith normal note values. The subject is then stated
ith normal note values in stretto with the answer in
iminution, the answer entering below the subject
fter one measure, all in F Major.

Section V. The subject in normal note values is
ombined in stretto with the answer, the answer entering
fter one measure above the subject, back in D Minor.

DIVISION TWO
Ms. 35-79

Section I. The answer is stated in what might be
alled its own exposition, in normal note values, with
he remaining three statements in diminution. The
irst three statements create a three-voice stretto in
Minor. The fourth statement is separated from the
irst statement by a brief episode, which also occurred
n the first section of Division One. The fourth
tatement is presented in B-flat Major.

Section II. The answer in normal note values is
ombined in stretto with the subject in diminution, the
ubject entering above the answer after one measure.
he two statements are in D Minor.

Section III. The answer in normal note values is
ombined in stretto with two statements of the subject
n diminution, all statements in D Minor.

Section IV. The answer in normal note values is
ombined with two statements of the subject in dim-
nution, the first statement of the subject being in F
ajor, and the second in D Minor. The answer is stated
n D Minor.

Section V. The answer in normal note values is
ombined with two statements of the subject in dim-
nution, all in G Minor, for the coda.

In both Division One and Division Two, Sections I

and III combine three-voice stretto statements in variou
combinations. Sections I and III have the voices
entering after the same number of measures in both
divisions. The last two sections of Division Two creat
an overlapping three-voice stretto of one beat.

An outline of the three-voice stretto statements
follows:

DIVISION ONE
Section I

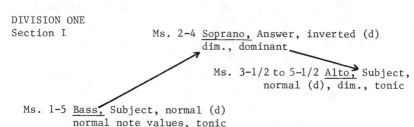

Ms. 2-4 <u>Soprano,</u> Answer, inverted (d)
dim., dominant

Ms. 3-1/2 to 5-1/2 <u>Alto,</u> Subject,
normal (d), dim., tonic

Ms. 1-5 <u>Bass,</u> Subject, normal (d)
normal note values, tonic

THREE VOICES SOUNDING TOGETHER IN MS. 3-1/2
TO 4, A TOTAL OF THREE BEATS.

Section III

Ms. 16-1/2 to 18-1/2 <u>Soprano,</u>
Answer, inverted (d),
dim., dominant

Ms. 16-20 <u>Tenor,</u> Subject, normal (d)
normal, tonic

Ms. 15-17 <u>Bass,</u> Answer, inverted (d)
dim., dominant

THREE VOICES SOUNDING TOGETHER IN MS. 16-1/2 TO
17-1/2, A TOTAL OF FOUR BEATS, WITH BASS LAST NOTE
EXTENDED TO A HALF NOTE, OTHERWISE THREE BEATS.

DIVISION TWO
Section I

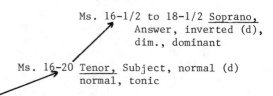

Ms. 35-39 <u>Soprano,</u> Answer, inverted (g)
normal note values, dominant

Ms. 37-1/2 to 39-1/2 <u>Tenor,</u>
Answer, inverted (g),
dim., dominant

Ms. 36-38 <u>Bass,</u> Subject, normal (g)
dim., tonic

THREE VOICES SOUNDING TOGETHER IN MS. 37-1/2 TO

76

38, A TOTAL OF THREE BEATS.

Section III

Ms. 57-59 <u>Soprano,</u> Subject, normal (d)
    dim., tonic

      Ms., 58-62 <u>Alto,</u> Answer, inverted (d)
        normal note values, dominant

           Ms. 58-1/2 to 60-1/2 <u>Tenor,</u>
             Subject, normal (d), dim.,
             tonic

     THREE VOICES SOUNDING TOGETHER IN MS. 58-1/2 TO
     59, A TOTAL OF THREE BEATS

   In Sections IV and V in Division Two, the three
voices sound together for but one beat, first in
M. 65-1/2 and then in M. 76-1/2. These one-beat three-
voice stretto statements result from the overlapping of
the two subject statements in diminution.

   The B begins the first two three-voice stretto
sections in Division One, while the S begins the second
two in Division Two.

   The subject and answer are combined in invertible
counterpoint with normal note values and in diminution.

   A more detailed study of the pivot Section IV
leading to an emphasis on the answer in stretto follows. By stating the answer in normal note values
before the subject in M. 20-1/2, a gradual transition
to the emphasis on the answer occurs.

SEC. IV	Ms. 20-24	Tenor	<u>Answer, inverted</u>	F
	Ms. 25-29	Alto	<u>Subject, normal</u>	F
	Ms. 26-28	Tenor	Answer, inverted, dim.	F
SEC. V	Ms. 31-35	Tenor	<u>Subject, normal</u>	d
	Ms. 32-34	Alto	Answer, inverted, dim.	d
(DIV. TWO) SEC. I	Ms. 35-39	Soprano	<u>Answer, inverted</u>	g

77

The subject and answer underlined above indicate the statements in normal note values. The entrance of the S answer at the beginning of Division Two in M. 35 is prepared by this sequence of statements.

Five episodes exist in both divisions. The style is "in stile Francese", having varying rhythmic figures depending on the prevailing performance practice of notes inégales.

Each of the stretto statements of the subject or answer is combined with a second or third voice in varying combinations and distances.

Contrapunctus VII: Contrapunctus VII states the subject and answer with normal note values, in diminution, and in augmentation.

The division of the fugue into six sections is governed by the four statements in augmentation.

The subject is stated primarily in normal order, but occurs twice in inverted order, both orders beginning and ending on the tonic. The answer is stated primarily in inverted order, beginning and ending on the dominant, but occurs once in inverted order, beginning and ending on the tonic. The distinction between the subject stated in inverted order, and the answer in inverted order, both beginning and ending on the tonic, can be made from the subject ending with c-sharp. and the answer ending with c-natural.

The four statements in augmentation are stated by each of the four voices in the following order:

Ms. 5-13(1/2)	B	Answer	inverted	d	tonic
Ms. 23-31	T	Subject	normal	F	tonic
Ms. 35-43	A	Answer	inverted	d	dominant
Ms. 50-58	S	Subject	normal	d	tonic

The four statements with normal note values are stated by three of the voices in the following order:

Ms. 2-6	S	Answer	inverted	d	dominant
Ms. 14-18	A	Answer	inverted	g	dominant
Ms. 36-40	T	Subject	normal, altered	d	tonic

78

Ms. 38-42   S   Subject   normal   d   tonic

Sections I, III, IV, and VI include statements of the subject or answer in augmentation. Sections II and V seem transitional between the more complex sections.

The exposition in Section I includes all three versions of the subject in normal, diminution, and augmentation. Section II relieves the tension of the complex stretto sections by stating two statements of the subject in diminution at the beginning and ending of the answer with normal note values.

Section III has two introductory statements of the subject and answer in diminution, leading directly to the augmented statement of the subject. Two additional statements of the subject and answer in diminution form a three-voice stretto with the subject in augmentation at the beginning of its statement, as do two final statements of the subject in diminution create a three-voice stretto with the subject in augmentation at the end of its statement.

The answer in augmentation begins Section IV, placed in three-voice stretto with two statements of the subject with normal note values. The last two statements of the answer in diminution overlap with the ending of the answer in augmentation. These last two statements of the answer in diminution in Section V begin a series of statements in diminution, progressing S A A T B, and lead to Section VI.

Section V is similar to Section II in that it seems as a transition from the highly complex stretto areas in Sections IV and VI.

Section VI states the subject in augmentation accompanied by one statement of the subject in stretto at the beginning of its subject, and accompanied by two tight stretto statements of the subject in diminution at the end of its statement.

In all of these sections, the distances after which a second or third voice follows a first voice varies, resulting in different combinations of stretto in each section.

Sections I, II, and III are divided from Sections IV, V, and VI by the longest episode. Sections II and V are similar in nature, and Sections III and VI have comparable conclusions:

			Section III				Section VI
M.	23-1/2	T	Subject, aug., normal	M.	50	S	Subject, aug., normal
M.	24-1/2	S	Answer, dim., inverted	M.	51	A	Subject, inverted, dim.
M.	28	B	Subject, dim., normal	M.	54-3/4	A	Subject, dim., normal
M.	29-1/2	A	Subject, dim., normal	M.	55	T	Subject, dim., normal

While the general scheme of statement of subject and answer in Section III is followed by Section VI, th subject is heard in all four statements in Section VI, even the inverted statement, as occurred in the exposition in M. 3. The end of Section VI shows a tightening of the stretto, resulting in a different stretto combination, and permitting the S in augmentation to complete its statement by itself, as did the B in augmentation complete the exposition by itself.

The A has three successive statements of the answe and subject from Ms. 35 to 47, spanning Sections IV and V.

Neither the subject nor the answer is stated by itself, in its entirety. Numerous stretto statements exist. The three-voice stretto statements continue for a longer period of time than occurred for the three-voice stretto sections in Contrapunctus VI.

Each of the three-voice stretto statements of this fugue is written with a different combination of voices note values, and distances of entrances. In Section I three-voice stretto occurs for one beat only on the first beats of M. 3, M. 5, and M. 9. All these statements will be considered two-voice stretto statements in this study, rather than three-voice stretto statements for one beat, similar to the analysis for the last two sections in Contrapunctus VI. No three-voice stretto statements exist in either Section II or Sectic V.

An analysis of the three-voice stretto statements in Sections III, IV, and VI follows.

SECTION III

Ms. 24-1/2 to 26-1/2 Soprano, Answer, inverted (F) dim., dominant

(Ms. 23-25 Alto,...)

80

Ms. 23-25 <u>Alto,</u> Subject, normal (F) (♩.)
      dim., tonic

          Ms. 23-1/2 (23-1/4) to 27 ... ,
              <u>Tenor,</u> Subject, normal (F)
              augmented, tonic

     THREE VOICES SOUNDING TOGETHER IN MS. 24-1/2 TO
     25-1/4, A TOTAL OF THREE BEATS.

             Ms. 29-1/2 to 31-1/2 <u>Alto,</u>
                Subject, normal (d)
                dim., tonic

Ms. ... 28 to 31 <u>Tenor,</u> Subject, normal (F)
      augmented, tonic

          Ms. 28-30 <u>Bass,</u> Subject, normal (d)
            dim., tonic

     THREE VOICES SOUNDING TOGETHER IN MS. 29-1/2 TO
     30-1/4, A TOTAL OF THREE BEATS.

SECTION IV   Ms. 38-1/4 to 42, <u>Soprano,</u>
                Subject, normal note
                values (d), normal order,
                tonic

Ms. 35-42 ... <u>Alto,</u> Answer, inverted (d)
      augmented, dominant

          Ms. 36-1/2 to 40-1/2 <u>Tenor,</u> Subject, normal
            (d), normal note values, tonic

     THIS IS THE LONGEST THREE-VOICE STRETTO STATEMENT
     IN THE STRETTO FUGUES. THREE VOICES SOUND
     TOGETHER IN MS. 38-1/4 to 41 (40-1/2), A
     TOTAL OF THREE MEASURES.

SECTION VI

Ms. ... 54-58 <u>Soprano,</u> Subject, normal (d)
      aug., tonic

          Ms. 54-3/4 to 56-3/4 <u>Alto,</u> Subject, normal
            (d), dim., tonic (e)

             Ms. 55-57 <u>Tenor,</u> Subject, normal
               (g), modified, dim.,
               tonic (a)

THREE VOICES SOUNDING TOGETHER IN MS. 55
TO 56 (57), A TOTAL OF TWO FULL MEASURES
(AND ONE BEAT).

In Section III the first three-voice stretto combines the subject in augmentation with two statements
of the subject and answer in diminution above it. The
subject in diminution is followed by the answer in
diminution in inverted order, after 1-1/2 measures. In
the second three-voice stretto in Section III, the T
subject in augmentation, starting with the sixth measure
of the subject, is joined by the B subject in diminution
below it, and the A subject in diminution above it, both
in normal order. The second statement of the subject
in diminution follows the first statement of the subject
in diminution after 1-1/2 measures, the same distance as
the two voices in diminution in the first three-voice
stretto of this section. The longest three-voice
stretto in Section IV creates a well-written three-part
counterpoint. The three-voice stretto is planned with
the A answer in inversion, with the remaining two voices
added below and above it, stating the subject with normal note values. Following the A answer in augmentation
the second and third voices enter after 1-1/2 measures,
the first note of the S subject in M. 38 being altered
to a quarter note.

In the last three-voice stretto in Section VI, the
last part of the S subject in augmentation and in normal
order is combined with two statements of the S in diminution. The first subject in diminution enters at
M. 54(3/4), and the second subject in diminution enters
one beat later at M. 55, the sixth measure of the subject in augmentation. This three-voice stretto differs
from the three-voice stretto in Section III occurring
at the end of the subject in augmentation, in that this
last three-voice stretto shows a tightening of the
stretto of the voices in diminution.

For all the triple or three-voice stretto statements, two versions of the subject or answer are combined, not three.

The three-voice stretto statements are planned to
progress from three three-voice sections for one beat
in the first section; to two three-voice stretto statements for three beats in Section III; to two lengthy
three-voice stretto statements in Sections IV and VI,
having three measures and two measures in stretto,
respectively. The three-voice stretto statements in
Sections IV and VI are the longest in the three stretto

fugues, and serve as a fitting conclusion to these
fugues.

Countrapunctus VII has a high degree of movement
throughout, achieved by few short episodes, continuous
stretto usage, and an emphasis on a four-part texture.
Tension is relieved by a reduction in the stretto complexity.

Sections I through III create a unit and begin and
end in D Minor, with modulations briefly to A Minor, then
G Minor, B-flat Major, F Major, and back to D Minor.
Sections IV through VI are a unit, and begin and end in
D Minor, with modulations to G Minor, F Major, and a
modified reference to G Minor at the end of Section VI.

THE DOUBLE AND TRIPLE FUGUES

Contrapunctus VIII: Division One emphasizing Subject I ends in D Minor with a definitive cadence in
M. 39. Subject II in double counterpoint with Subject
I begins immediately with M. 39, serving as the beginning of Division Two. Section IV in Division Two
has three double counterpoint statements of Subjects I
and II, in F Major, B-flat Major, and D Minor. A
climactic cadence rounds off Division Two emphasizing
Subject II, with running sixteenth notes and thirty-
second notes for heightened climax, ending in D Minor in
M. 93. The cadence does not end with all voices, as at
the end of Division One. The B continues in M. 93 with
motives similar to M. 17. M. 93 ends on the dominant
of D Minor, returning to the tonic in D Minor in M. 94
with the entrance of Subject III. Although the entrance
of Subject III is not so clearly defined as the entrances of Subjects I and II, the entire presentation
of Subject III forms the most complete fughetta of the
three subjects. Section VI has two stretto statements
of Subjects I and II in D Minor and combined D Minor and
A Minor. Section VI ends in A minor in M. 135.

No definitive cadence or partially-definitive
cadence occurs before the first of the final triple
counterpoint statements of the three subjects. An
overlapping of phrases takes place, appropriately
introducing the triple counterpoint statements of all
three subjects.

Following Section VI, all three subjects are stated
in triple counterpoint with varying combinations of
voices, each in invertible counterpoint. The four
triple counterpoint statements in Section VII occur in

F Major, F Major with modulations, G Minor, and back to
D Minor. Except for Section VIIB, all three subjects
are presented in the same key in each triple counterpoint statement. Episodes occur between each triple
counterpoint statement in Section VII.

A study of the procedures for combining the three
subjects reveals the careful planning by Bach of the
invertible contrapuntal combinations of the three subjects.

TRIPLE COUNTERPOINT I

    Section VIIA   S   Subject I   F
                      A   Subject II   F
                      B   Subject III F, modulates

TRIPLE COUNTERPOINT II

    Section VIIB   A   Answer I F (C)
                      B   Answer II F (C)
                      S   Answer III g, modulates

TRIPLE COUNTERPOINT III

    Section VIIC   B   Subject I   g
                      S   Subject II   g
                      A   Subject III g

TRIPLE COUNTERPOINT IV

    Section VIID   B   Subject I   d
                      A   Subject II   d
                      S   Subject III d

In the statements in triple counterpoint I and II,
all three statements are tonal. In triple counterpoint
III and IV, all three statements are real, with the
exception of a concluding e-flat in Subject II in M.
172. By keeping the statements of the three subjects
in the same order in the above listing, it can be seen
that the four triple statements have varying combinations of voices, but are planned in a symmetrical way.
Section VIIA is reversed in Section VIID. The A begins
Section VIIB but ends Section VIIC; the B and S have
interchanged subjects in these same two sections. The
S states Subjects I, II, and III, and Answer III. The
A states Subject II twice, Subject III, and Answer I.
The B states Subject I twice, Subject III, and Answer
II. All three voices state the three subjects.

The final triple counterpoint in Section VIII serves also as the coda. The order of voices and subjects is now the same as triple counterpoint I, Section VIIA, but in D Minor, rather than F Major as in Section VIIA.

TRIPLE COUNTERPOINT V

Section VIII	S	Subject I	d
	A	Subject II	d
	B	Subject III	d

All voices stating the three subjects in the coda are basically real.

A reduction in voices in this fugue is not the only way used to lessen tension. The tension is varied also between the texture of the single, double, and triple statements, and the imitative motivic texture of the episodes.

Subject II is combined with Subject I for every statement. Subject III is included in four triple counterpoint statements, but does not appear in double counterpoint with either of the other two subjects.

Countrapunctus IX: The first double fugue is written in double counterpoint at the twelfth (alla Duodecima). When Subject I is placed above Subject II, Subject I is a fifth higher; below Subject II, Subject I is based on counterpoint at the octave. This is the only way the double counterpoint appears in this fugue in both major and minor statements. Following the opening exposition for Subject I, both Subjects I and II are heard together for all successive entries.

An analysis of the entry of each subject reveals the independent structure of each. The order of entrances of Subject I is:

Section I	A	Section II	T	Section III	A
Exposition	S		A		
	B		B		
	T		A	Section IV	T
			S	Coda	

The last T voice of the exposition is the last voice heard in the coda.

Subject II begins after the exposition for Subject I, having the following entries:

Section I	Not	Section II	S	Section III	T
Exposition	heard		T		
			A		
			T	Section IV	A
			B	Coda	

The first entrance of voices for Subject II in Section II is circular, with A being the center voice. The A began Exposition I stating Subject I, and the A ends the coda as Subject II combined with T Subject I.

All double counterpoint entrances of Subject I with Subject II are combined after one beat. Since Subject begins on a weak beat, this double counterpoint combination seems natural. The combination of the two subjects does not vary in distance of entries. Althougl Subject I gives the appearance of a counter-subject whe: combined with Subject II, strict rules for entrances of the counter-subject are not followed.

In all the double counterpoint arrangements of Subject I with Subject II, no combinations of voices ar< repeated. Although Answer II is combined as T with A Answer I in Sections IIB and IID, Section IIB is in F Major, whereas Section IID is in A Minor.

Contrapunctus X: Contrapunctus X is written in double counterpoint at the tenth (alla Decima), with parallel thirds used with both subjects. Both subjects are stated in invertible counterpoint an octave or tentl below or above the other subject, resulting from usage of parallel statements in double counterpoint. Each of the two subjects in Contrapunctus X is first stated in its own division having its own exposition. Following the individual divisions, the two subjects are combined in double counterpoint with or without a third parallel voice.

The entire Contrapunctus X is planned as a stretto fugue. No subject or answer is heard completely by itself. Subject I is new, and Subject II is the same as the subject of the stretto fugues, which augments the emphasis on stretto structure, as does the close integration of the episodes and free material.

Subject I and Answer I are stated in normal and inverted orders. All statements of Subject II and Answer II are in inverted order. The first three voice: in Exposition I are the same three voices combined in double counterpoint with added parallel voice to end the fugue. Following the first two divisions, Subject

I or Answer I is always heard in some form of double
counterpoint with Subject II or Answer II. The same
relationship of Subject I to a counter-subject for
Subject II can be seen here as was observed in Contrapunctus IX, although strict rules for the entrance of
a counter-subject are not followed.

Contrapunctus XI: Four separate divisions are
required to present the three subjects, since Subject I
has its own division and exposition for both the normal
and inverted orders. Subject II is stated with a new
counter-subject rather than the counter-subject which
exists in Contrapunctus VIII as Subject II.

In Section VI, Subject II is stated with Subject III
as a counter-subject, as occurred in Contrapunctus VIII.
In Contrapunctus XI, Subject II is presented with two
statements of Subject III, rather than but one statement
of this subject as was seen in M. 39 of Contrapunctus
VIII. Subject III in this fugue is first presented in
retrograde version of Subject II of Contrapunctus VIII.
Section VI serves a double function: that of presenting Subject II with the more familiar counter-subject,
Subject III; and presenting Subject III as a separate
subject in various stretto combinations. In this Contrapunctus XI, Subject III is presented both with Subjects I and II. Section VII continues to present Subject III in varying stretto combinations. The first
counter-subject for Subject II is heard with Subject III
in Section VII. Numerous intermediate sections stress
Subject III.

One statement of Subject I by the B in normal order
is stated in Section VIII, which concludes Division Four.
Similar one-voice statements occur at the ends of
Division One and Division Two.

The second double counterpoint statement with a
parallel third voice in Section IX has a similar procedure to the first double counterpoint statement in
Section VIA, but the voices are changed, as follows:

Section VIA, Ms. 89 to 93

Subject II	B	inverted	dominant	d
Subject III	T	retrograde	supertonic (flat)	d
Subject III	A	retrograde	submediant (flat)	d

Section IX, Ms. 136 to 140

Subject II	T	inverted	dominant	d
Subject III	A	retrograde	supertonic (flat)	d
Subject III	S	retrograde	dominant	d

Section X includes the first triple counterpoint in which all three subjects are stated simultaneously.

Section XI states Subject III, Subject I, and Answer I in mirror stretto, respectively. Sections XIIA and XIIB in the coda complete the three triple counterpoint sections. All three subjects are presented in the same order in these last two triple counterpoint statements, but by different voices, in D Minor. All three subjects are stated in invertible counterpoint with each other, and three different voices present the three statements of each subject.

The start of the B Subject II in the coda in M. 174 overlaps Episode (19) with the coda over a deceptive cadence to the submediant, so that a definitive cadence does not usher in the coda. The last triple counterpoint statement in the fugue in Section XIIB states all three subjects as initially stated in their respective expositions in this second triple fugue, in the sequence from S to B. Subject I is stated by the S, rather than the A as appeared in Exposition I, adding brilliance to the final triple counterpoint. Several minor exceptions to the initial statements occur: Subject II in the T begins with a quarter note, and Subject III is tonally modified and abbreviated.

A reduction in voices is not used to lessen the tension nor to create dynamic changes. The three (four) expositions begin with a reduction in voices, but other than these sections, Contrapunctus XI remains basically in a four-voice structure.

Increased tension, harmonic coloring, dynamic density - these are achieved by tighter stretto sections, chromaticism, dense usage of motives, and the number of subjects in stretto and double and triple counterpoint.

Subject III is given considerable contrapuntal interest in this Contrapunctus XI. Subject III is stated in innumerable stretto combinations, including four-voice stretto in intermediate sections. Four intermediate sections emphasize Subject III. The four-voice stretto sections base all motivic material on

Subject III. Many of these statements of Subject III
are fairly complete, so that these sections have more
weight than mere episodes. The four intermediate
sections occur in the following measures:

Intermediate Section (A)
Ms. 111-3/4 to 114, 4 voices

The false entry of Subject III in normal order in
the B leads to the last stretto statement of Subject III
in Section VI. The three voices above the B false entry
continue the material begun in Episode (11). The false
entry of Subject III is the only individual statement
of Subject III within this fugue.

Intermediate Section (B)
Ms. 130-1/4 to 132-1/2, 4 voices

Although the T begins a motivic passage based on
Subject III in M. 129, the four-voice stretto begins in
M. 130-1/4. The entire Section is in D Minor. Few notes
in all four voices are not based on motives taken from
Subject III. The B and T are in normal order, while the
S and A are in inverted order. M. 131 appears as a
mirror stretto between the upper two and lower two
voices.

Intermediate Section (B) could be said to be a
tightening of the stretto statements of Subject III
presented in Section VII.

Intermediate Section (C)
Ms. 140-1/4 to 144, 4 voices

All four voices present some form of Subject III
in imitation in pairs, the paired imitation being based
on the A and S statements of Subject III in Section IX.
All four voices are in D Minor.

The normal statement of Subject III in the T is
imitated in stretto by the inverted B statement. The
S normal statement is next imitated in stretto by the
A normal statement. The four voices do not continue in
as strict stretto as occurred in Intermediate Section
(B); however, the imitation in pairs is clearly defined.

Intermediate Section (D)
Ms. 167-3/4 to 172-1/4, 4 voices

Following the three mirror stretto statements in
Section XI, Intermediate Section (D) continues the

mirror idea, but based only on Subject III and in paire
mirror imitation. All four voices are basically in D
Minor, although the A modulates to G Minor in M. 169-1/

The inverted statement of Subject III is first
stated by the S, imitated in stretto by the A in retrograde inversion. Next follows the T inverted statement, imitated in stretto by the B in normal order.

THE FOUR CANONS

Each of the four canons has its own procedure and
time signature, and may be said to draw upon some of th
techniques of the fugue. Three of the canons have a
new, elaborated subject based on the original fugue
subject. The fourth canon has a rhythmically-altered
variant of the fugue subject as its subject.

The four canons are so expanded structurally that
numerous procedures of the fugues can be found in the
process of their completion. Since each of the canons
is constructed differently, the same fugal procedures
do not necessarily exist in each canon.

The sequence of entrances of the subjects in each
of the four canons can find parallels in the sequence
of voices in the fugues. The entrance of the second
voice in each of the canons is either real or tonal,
as is the case with the fugues. The entrances of the
second voice might be called "Answers". In contrapunctus XIV from M. 79 to the end, this concluding section has many similarities to the codas in the fugues.
A pedal point exists in the lower voice before the fina
cadence. Increased rhythmic interest is added to the
upper voice for climactic purposes. The lower voice
modifies the length of the subject by presenting it in
diminution. The ending of Contrapunctus XIV summarizes
the procedures in the canon as a coda would do.

Contrapuncti XII and XV adhere most closely to
strict canonic procedures. Canons found in Contrapuncti XIII and XIV have a basic canonic structure, but
are not exact in their completion. Contrapuncti XIII
and XIV might be called two-part fugues, although a two
part fugue need not follow such a strict canonic
procedure.

While we cannot be sure of Bach's intention for
including the canons in Die Kunst der Fuge, or whether
these canons are strictly speaking part of this work, w
find some interesting correlations between the canons

90

nd the fugues. The usage of the subject of Die Kunst
ler Fuge for the canons shows a direct relation to this
ork. Also, is it possible Bach was seeking procedures
f the canon that could be applied to the fugue, and
ice versa? Bach does include canonic episodes in his
ugues. Any two voices in the exposition of a fugue,
hether simple, double, triple, stretto, or mirror,
ould have a resemblance to a two-part canon, especially
ith a real counter-subject. Within a fugue structure,
he subject or answer could be presented in canon at
trategic moments, such as intermediate sections, with
he free material and episodes retaining a canonic
tructure.

ONTRAPUNCTUS XII:

Contrapunctus XII is a canon alla ottava after four
easures, beginning with the upper voice, in 9/16 meter,
he subject starting and ending on the dominant.

The first part of the canon subject is an elabora-
ion of the original fugue subject of this study. The
econd part of the canon subject intricately alters
he rhythm of the original fugue subject.

rocedure of the Canon, Ms. 1-103

Contrapunctus XII is an exact canon or strict
anon from M. 1 to the first beat of M. 99. The new
aterial added in the upper voice from here to the
nd completes the first voice. The canon is divided
nto two sections. The first section, Ms. 1-80, is
epeated. The second section, Ms. 81 to the end, begins
s the first section with voice parts reversed. Ms.
1-99 are the same as Ms. 5-23, with parts reversed. In
s. 99-103, the lower voice continues as the lower
oice in Ms. 23-27, and thus has no new material. To
omplete the canon, new material is added to the upper
oice in Ms. 99-103, based on motives from the canon.
eats 2 and 3 in M. 100 are similar to beats 2 and 3 in
. 32, in the upper voice. The last two measures of
he upper voice are planned with rests and leaps to
reate a cadential effect.

Contrapunctus XII has four statements of the canon
ubject presented in the upper voice, imitated in the
ower voice:

MEASURE NOS. (Upper Voice)	MEASURE NOS. (Lower Voice)	ORDER	STARTING NOTE	KEY
1-5	5-9	inverted	dominant	d
25-29	29-33	inverted	tonic	d
41-45	45-59	normal	tonic	d
77-81	81-85	inverted	dominant	d

Cadential material concludes the measures preceding each new subject entry. Frequently rests occur
in the voice presenting the subject in anticipation
of its statement. New, decisive entries begin in the
upper voice in Ms. 52 and 61, which seem to be based
on motives from the canon subject.

Sequence is frequently found in one voice, as in
Ms. 7-8, and in Ms. 33-34, in the upper voice, followed
after four measures by the lower voice.

CONTRAPUNCTUS XIII:

Contrapunctus XIII is a canon alla duodecima in
contrapuncto alla quinta after eight measures, beginning with the lower voice, in ¢ meter, the subject
(with sextuplet figures) starting and ending on the
tonic.

The canon subject is based on the normal order of
the original fugue subject. The first note of each
measure in Ms. 1-7 states the original fugue subject,
and the canon subject is expanded around this outline.
The remaining notes of the fugue subject occur on
weak stresses of the canon subject in Ms. 7-1/2 to 9.

The subject has a rhythmic lilt because of the
six-note figures in the first measure. These sextuplet figures permit colorful rhythmic contrasts within
the body of the canon. Few melodic skips occur in the
subject, with the noteable exception of the descending
diminished seventh in M. 5, serving as the end of the
first phrase of the subject. The subject can be
divided into two phrases: Ms. 1 to 5-1/2 and 5-1/2 to
9. The last phrase can be subdivided into Ms. 5-1/2 to
7-1/2 and 7-1/2 to 9. Several sequences occur in the
subject.

Procedure of the Canon, Ms. 1-78

92

The procedure of the entire canon depends upon little material that is not repeated by both voices. Following the statement of the canon subject by the lower voice, Ms. 9-75 are repeated. New material is added to both voices to complete the cadence in Ms. 76-79. A summary of the procedure of Contrapunctus XIII follows:

MEASURE NOS. (Lower Voice)	MEASURE NOS. (Upper Voice)	SOURCE OF MATERIAL	DISTANCE OF THE CANON
Ms. 1-26		original canon	
	9-34	"answer" of original canon	at the 12th (5th) above
Ms. 26-35		same as upper voice, Ms. 59-68	
Ms. 34-42		same as upper voice, Ms. 68-76	
	34-68	original canon, Ms. 1-35, lower voice	
Ms. 42-67		"answer" of original canon, Ms. 9-34	at two octaves (octave) below, invertible cpt.
Ms. 68-76		original canon subject, same as lower voice, Ms. 1-9	
	68-76	same as lower voice, Ms. 34-42 (5th higher)	
Ms. 77-79	77-79	voices proceed freely to complete canon	

The canon does not continue with the initial voices in canon at the 12th (5th), but proceeds by invertible canon at M. 34 by canon at the octave. The lower voice is the first voice in M. 1; the upper voice is the first voice in M. 34; the lower voice returns to the original canon subject and becomes the first voice in M. 68. The return to canon at the 12th occurs in M. 68 in the upper voice. The upper voice had been stating the original canon in Ms. 34-68. Ms. 67 of the upper voice was the same as M. 34 of the lower voice. The upper voice in M. 68 then repeats M. 34 in the lower voice, and the repetition of M. 34 in M. 68 is a fifth higher. The upper voice continues in Ms. 68-76 to repeat the entire Ms. 34-42 of the lower voice, a fifth higher. The last few measures draw upon motives of the canon in imitation and sequence to bring Contrapunctus XIII to a close.

All major presentations of the first eight-measure subject in either voice are real or exact. The rest of the canon is tonal, having chromatic altera-tions in the second voice to accommodate changes in tonality.

CONTRAPUNCTUS XIV:

Contrapunctus XIV is a canon alla decima contra-puncto alla terza, after four measures, beginning with the lower voice, in C $\frac{12}{8}$ meter. The subject is the same as the original subject of Die Kunst der Fuge, but rhythmically altered. The rhythmically altered canon subject is presented in diminution at the end of the canon as the final entrance of the canon sub-ject.

The entrance of the second voice or "Answer" in M. 5 is tonal in F Major, the relative major of D Minor, and begins and ends on the dominant, inverted. The resulting tonal contrasts between the minor key and its relative major in this canon at the tenth create unique contrapuntal procedures.

Procedure of the Canon, Ms. 1-83

The entire canon is tonal, including the state-ments of the subject. Little material exists that is not heard in both voices. No major section is repeated with repeat marks, as occurred in the previous two canons. A summary of the procedure of Contrapunctus XIV follows:

MEASURE NOS. (Lower Voice)	MEASURE NOS. (Upper Voice)	SOURCE OF MATERIAL	DISTANCE OF THE CANON
Ms. 1-35		original canon	
	5-39	"answer" of original canon	at the 10th (3rd) above
Ms. 36-39		same as upper voice, Ms. 75-78, both	

94

MEASURE NOS. (Lower Voice)	MEASURE NOS. (Upper Voice)	SOURCE OF MATERIAL	DISTANCE OF THE CANON
(continued)			
		sections necessary to complete the second voice	
Ms. 40-43		(see description below)	
	40-74	original canon, same as lower voice, Ms. 1-35	
Ms. 44-78		"answer" of original canon, but similar to lower voice, Ms. 1-35	at the octave
Ms. 79-81		subject of canon in diminution	
	75-78	same as lower voice, Ms. 36-39	
	79-83	new material and intricate rhythmic complexity for climax	
Ms. 81-83		basically a pedal point conclusion	

Ms. 40-43 in the lower voice are based on Ms. 5-7 in the lower voice, with the addition of a cadential measure with new material, climactically leading to the return to the subject in the lower voice in M. 44. The beginning of Ms. 40, 41, and 42 have added sixteenth notes for contrast.

In Ms. 79-83 in the upper voice, a coda might be inferred because of the progressively more intricate rhythmic complexity, larger intervallic leaps, and increased melodic movement, all above the subject in diminution, followed by a pedal point.

The canon proceeds by invertible counterpoint, but the distance changes to an octave with the entrance of the original canon in the upper voice in Ms. 40-74. The "Answer" by the lower voice in Ms. 44-78 is based on the lower voice in Ms. 1-35, not the upper voice in Ms. 5-39, since it remains in D Minor.

95

Although the upper voice leads the canon starting in M. 40, the upper voice depends primarily upon the material presented by the lower voice. The main exception is the concluding cadential material in Ms. 79-83.

For the material not presented as canon subject, techniques of sequences of varying lengths, rhythmic variants, complete phrase endings, all add to the ultimate growth of the canon. Rhythm plays a large part in this canon. The syncopated beginning of the canon subject permits numerous suspensions and resolutions with the second voice. The dotted rhythm ending of the canon subject combines with the numerous triplets, following the rules of <u>notes inégales</u>.

Numerous varieties of rhythmic patterns appear in one voice. In the lower voice in Ms. 17-22, a measure in all quarter notes introduced by suspensions is contrasted to measures with triplet figures and sixteenth notes. Rhythmic patterns in sequence are frequent: in the lower voice in Ms. 15-16; Ms. 23-24; to name but a few. All the rhythmic complexities that exist in this canon are climaxed by the coda-like section at the end of the canon in Ms. 79-83. This brief section seems to embody much of the rhythmic interest of the entire canon, as a coda might do. The combinations of individual rhythms between the two voices lead to vertical and imitative rhythmic dimensions.

Chromaticism is used with discretion. In M. 19 in the lower voice, a descending chromatic line with all quarter notes is written to compensate harmonically for the lack of rhythmic interest in the consistent quarter notes.

A succession of wide skips, with or without dotted rhythm, is used for a climactic cadence, as in M. 39 in the upper voice, leading to its statement of the original canon in M. 40.

The concluding trill on the half note of beat 3 of M. 81 in the upper voice is similar to the half note trill in the measure with new material in M. 43 in the lower voice. Both trills augment the cadential ending.

The scheme of the entrances of the canon subject is:

MEASURE NOS. (Lower Voice)	MEASURE NOS. (Upper Voice)	ORDER	STARTING NOTE	KEY
1-5		inverted	dominant	d
	5-9	inverted	dominant	F
9-13		inverted	dominant	F
	13-17	inverted	dominant	a
	40-44	inverted	dominant	d
44-48		inverted	dominant	d
	48-52	inverted	dominant	F
52-56		inverted	dominant	F
79-81, presented in diminution		inverted	dominant	d

CONTRAPUNCTUS XV:

Contrapunctus XV is a canon per augmentationem in contrario motu, after four measures at the distance of a fourth starting with the upper voice, in ¢ meter. The upper voice begins on the tonic in normal order, while the lower voice begins on the dominant in inverted order in augmentation. When the two voices are reversed in M. 53, the lower voice begins on the tonic in normal order, and the upper voice begins on the dominant in inverted order.

The subject is an elaborated version of the original fugue subject. Rhythmic movement takes place on the first beat of every measure of the subject, while the second beat has a half note in every measure. The last beat has quarter notes or eighth notes as resolutions or passing notes. The half note on the second beat serves as a syncopated suspension in rhythm, permitting greater activity in the second voice during these beats. Especially is greater interest possible in the contrasting voice when the subject is presented in augmentation, as in Ms. 7-1/2 to 8-1/2 in the lower voice. The "Answer" states a tonal answer in augmentation and inversion starting on the dominant.

Procedure of the Canon, Ms. 1-109

The original canon presented by the upper voice is imitated by the lower voice in augmentation and inversion. Little material is presented beyond the basic canon. The augmented voice is able to present half the material of the original canon. Ms. 1-24 of the original canon in normal note values are stated in Ms. 5-52 in the lower voice in augmentation. The augmented lower voice proceeds immediately to its statement of the original canon in Ms. 53-106, which measures are the same as Ms. 1-54 in the upper voice. The augmented voice in Ms. 57-104 are the same as the previous lower voice in augmentation in Ms. 5-52. The upper voice continues in Ms. 105 to the end with one final statement of the canon subject with normal note values.

New material is stated at the end of the canon in the lower voice in Ms. 106 to 108, needed to complete the canon subject presented in the upper voice. This is the only new material in the entire canon. The new material is based on motives within the canon in sequence.

Although the canon is tonal throughout, an unusual procedure creates exact invertible counterpoint. From Ms. 1-53, the two voices proceed with tonal adjustments. At M. 53 the parts are reversed, but no further tonal adjustments are made beyond those presented in the first half of the canon. The canon proceeds in exact invertible counterpoint to M. 105. The material in the canon other than the subject shows an intricate degree of counterpoint. Motives from the rhythmically-complex subject are used in various ways. The syncopated half-note suspension of the second beat of the measure is used in augmentation, normal note values, and in diminution. This suspension occurs on a weak beat following a rhythmic figure on the strong beat in numerous varieties. Sequences of varying lengths occur. Because of the longer note values in the augmented voice, the voice with normal note values has more interest. Following M. 24, the measure which is the last to be imitated by the voice in augmentation, the original canon becomes especially flexible. This section is not answered, so the first voice takes advantage of its freedom of structure. Increased melodic movement takes place; short syncopated motives in sequence and in diminution occur; definite phrase endings are stated; and many contrasts in melodic design and rhythm occur. All these patterns are heard in the lower voice when the voices are reversed, without alterations to M. 106. The scheme of the entrance of the canon subject is:

MEASURE NOS. (Upper Voice)	MEASURE NOS. (Lower Voice)	ORDER (Note Values)	STARTING NOTE	KEY
1-5		normal order, normal note values	tonic	d
	5-13	inverted, aug.	dominant	d
	53-57	normal order, normal note values	tonic	d
57-65		inverted, aug.	dominant	d
105-109 (the end)		normal order, normal note values	tonic	d

THE TWO MIRROR FUGUES

CONTRAPUNCTUS XVI:

Contrapunctus XVI had five major sections. Sections I, III, and V are the most complete sections, with Sections I and III having all three voices presenting a statement of subject or answer. In the three main sections of Contrapunctus XVI, no episodes exist between the statements of the subject or answer. As one statement ends, the next begins on the same beat. Sections II and IV have one statement of the answer by the alto. Episodes exist before and after each statement.

The entry of the voices in Contrapunctus XVI, Rectus, follows the basic plan of A, B, and S, with the subject and answer consistently alternating. The one statement of the answer in Sections II and IV permits a change in the first voice in Sections III and V. The resulting sequence is as follows:

Section I	A	B	S	
	Subject	Answer	Subject	
Section II	A			
	Answer			
Section III		B	S	A
		Subject	Answer	Subject
Section IV	A			
	Answer			
Section V		B	S	
		Subject	Answer	

Without deviating from the scheme of "Subject",
"Answer", consistently alternating, the basic entry
of voices remains A, B, and S, with each of the three
voices stating both subject and answer.

A close integration exists between the major sections and the episodes. The last voice in statement
of subject or answer serves as the basis for imitation
or sequence in the ensuing episode. As an example, the
B in Ms. 13-14 imitates the last measure of the S
Subject in M. 12, the imitation being in normal and
inverted orders. The A is the voice that is imitated
in Episodes (2) through (4), since the A is the last
voice to state a subject or answer. The A in each
episode states the motive in the same direction as the
A subject or answer preceding the episode. The S in
the episode states the same motive in inversion,
resulting in imitation between A and S without interruption from the last statement of the subject, or
answer through the first part of the ensuing episode,
as in Ms. 23-27.

Lengthy rests that exist in any one voice prepare
for the next entrance of the subject or answer in the
same voice. Constant combinations of triplet figures
with dotted eighths and sixteenths would follow the
rules of notes inégales in performance.

Statements of the subject and answer occur in D
Minor in all sections except Section III, which
modulates to B-flat Major and G Minor. All statements
of the subject and answer begin with an upbeat.

All statements of the subject and answer are based
on the normal order of the original fugue subject of
this study. Three versions of this mirror fugue
subject are included in this one fugue. The subject
in the exposition has identical notes as the original
fugue subject, but varies in meter and rhythm. After
the exposition, all subsequent statements of the subject
are based on the original subject of Die Kunst der
Fuge in normal order, but the subject is elaborated.
The last statement of the subject in Section III has
the greatest amount of elaboration. The elaborated
version of the fugue subject in Sections II and III
begin with added ascending and descending four-note
figures. With the consistent use of the elaborated
form of the subject with eighth notes, the free
material and episodes become more dense with greater
eighth-note movement. Many imitative passages are
based on these four-note fugures.

The answer is not stated beyond the exposition.
The voices enter in reverse order from the order in the
exposition in Section II, all voices stating the subject, and being separated by episodes.

THE QUADRUPLE FUGUE
CONTRAPUNCTUS XVIII:

Bach was unable to complete Contrapunctus XVIII
before his death. If the fugue is considered an
integral part of Die Kunst der Fuge, what specific
fugal procedures are being added to those already
manifested in the first nineteen fugues?

Gustav Nottebohm (1817-1882) discovered that the
first three subjects in this fugue could be combined
with the original fugue subject of Die Kunst der Fuge,
thus permitting the completion of this fugue as a
quadruple fugue. Tovey believes that one quadruple
fugue was not the only intention of Bach. Tovey includes in his edition of Die Kunst der Fuge his own
conclusion of the quadruple fugue which Bach had
begun. Tovey further interprets Mizler's statement as
meaning an additional four-part fugue with four subjects as an ultimate finale, but being written as a
completely invertible mirror fugue. In this second
mirror fugue, Tovey retains the subject based on Bach's
name, combines this with a rhymically-altered form of
the subject of the stretto fugues, and adds two sub-

jects of his own.

Helmut Walcha includes his own conclusion to Contrapunctus XVIII, being based on quadruple counterpoint and written in a highly chromatic style.

Contrapunctus XVIII is frequently concluded with the chorale, "Wenn wir in höchsten Nöten sein", called by Bach "Vor deinen Thron tret ich hiermit", the setting of which was included at the end of the Original Edition. Bach presumably preferred the text by Bodo von Hodenberg of "Vor deinen Thron tret ich hiermit" to be sung to the chorale tune by Louis Bourgeois of "Wenn wir in höchsten Nöten sein". The chorale prelude included in the Original Edition of Die Kunst der Fuge is an expanded setting beyond that found in the Orgelbüchlein of "Wenn wir in höchsten Nöten sein". Charles Sanford Terry discusses the association of this chorale with Die Kunst der Fuge in his article entitled "Bach's Swan-Song" in MQ XIX (No. 3, July, 1933). Terry concludes the editors of the Original Edition included it to compensate purchasers for the incomplete score of Bach, and was not intended by Bach to be part of this work.

A copy of the extant Contrapunctus XVIII is made a part of Ferruccio Busoni's Fantasia Contrappuntistic

CONTRAPUNCTUS I
(a4) Ms. 1-78

I, Ms. 1-23

Exposition, Ms. 1-17

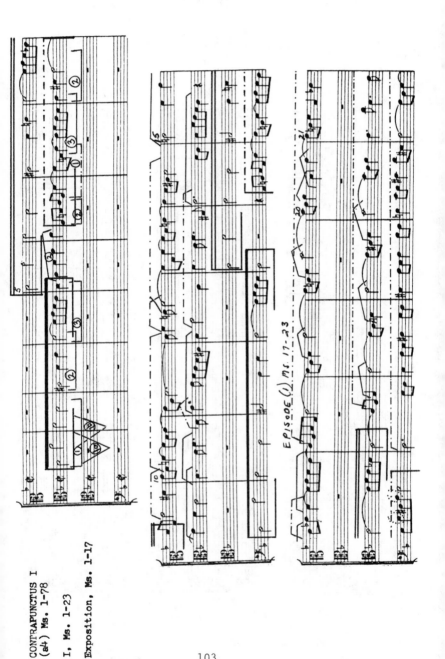

EPISODE (1) Ms. 17-23

103

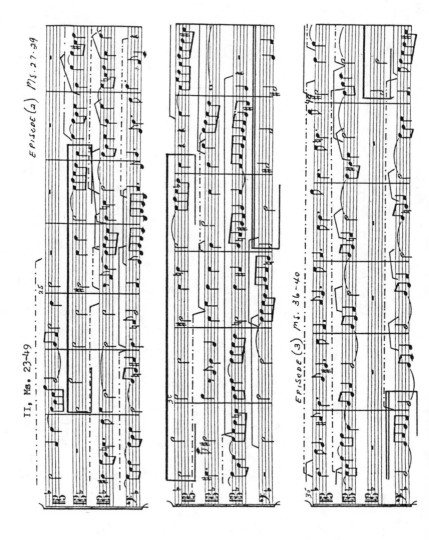

104

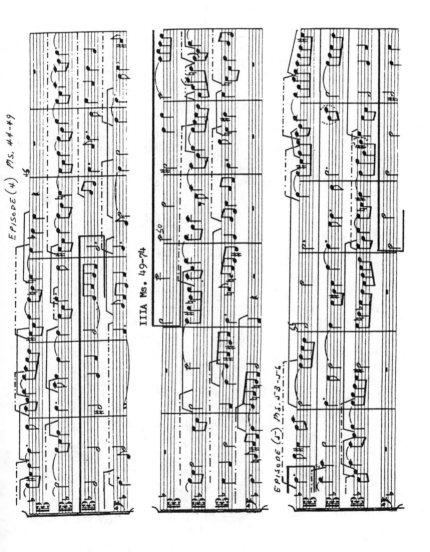

105

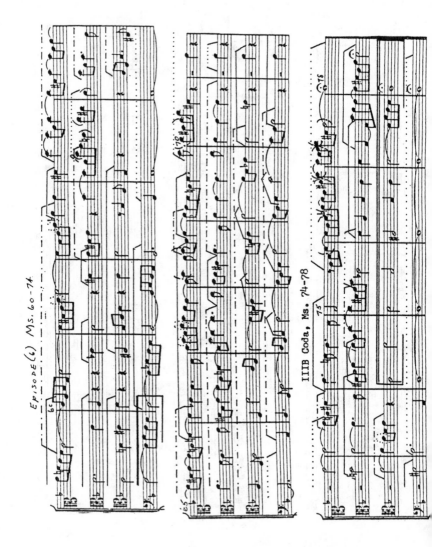

106

CONTRAPUNCTUS II
(a4) Ms. 1-84

I, Ms. 1-23

Exposition, Ms. 1-23

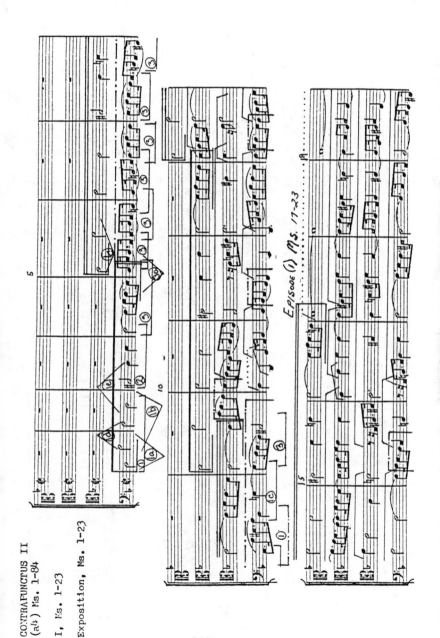

EPISODE (1) Ms. 17-23

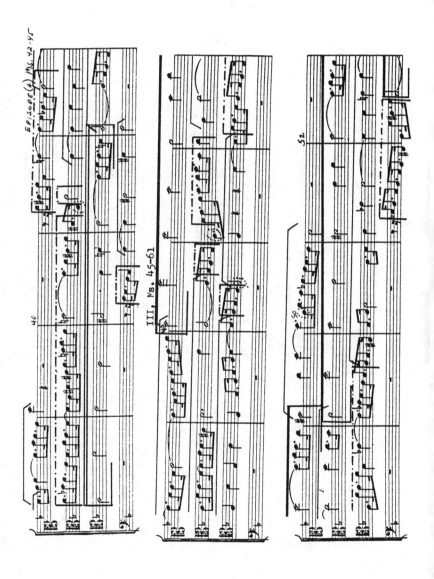

III, Ms. 45-61

109

IV, Ms. 61-79

111

Contrapunctus III
(a4) Ms. 1-72

I, Ms. 1 to 23-1/4

Exposition,
Ms. 1-19

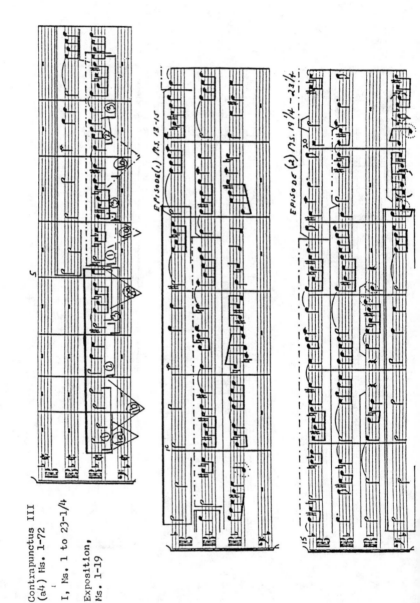

Intermediate Section (A), Ms. 23-1/4 to 43

EPISODE (3) Ms. 27-29 1/4

EPISODE (4) Ms. 33-35 1/4

113

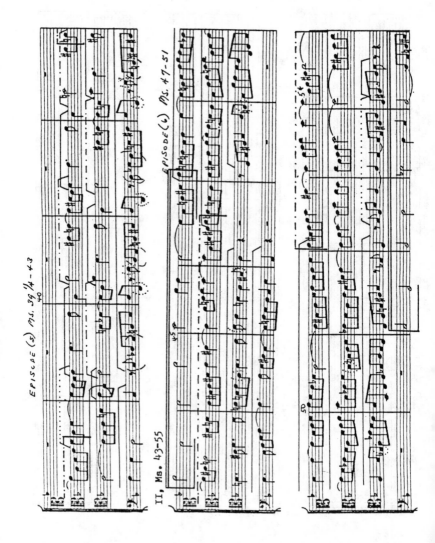

114

Intermediate Section (B), Ms. 55-62

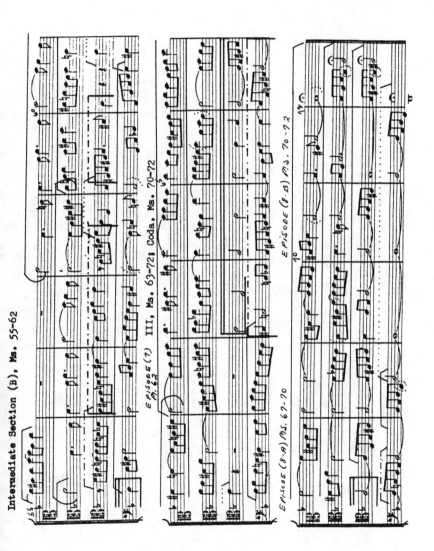

EPISODE (7) III, Ms. 63-72; Coda, Ms. 70-72

EPISODE (8-A) MS. 67-70

EPISODE (8-B) MS. 70-92

115

CONTRAPUNCTUS IV
(a4) Ms. 1-138

I, Ms. 1-27

Exposition, Ms. 1-19

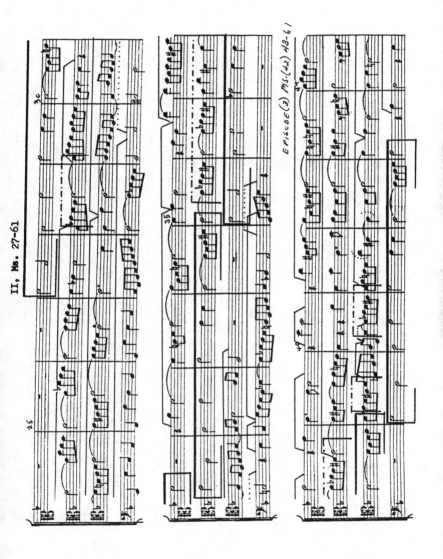

II, Ms. 27-61

EPISODE (3) Ms. (42) 43-61

III, Ms. 61-107

118

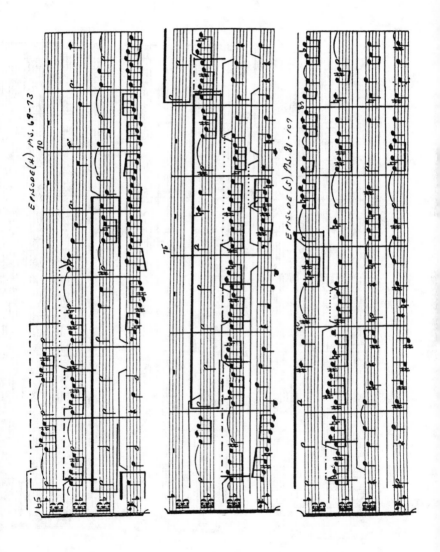

119

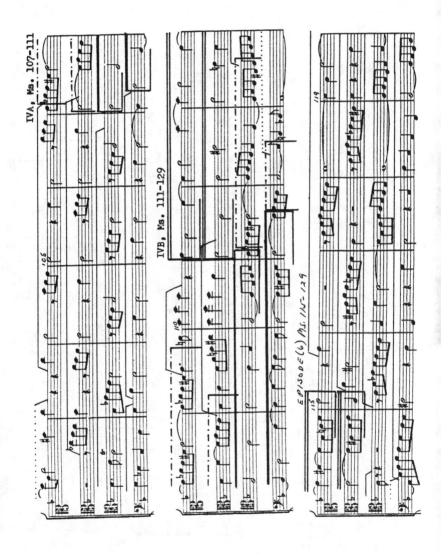

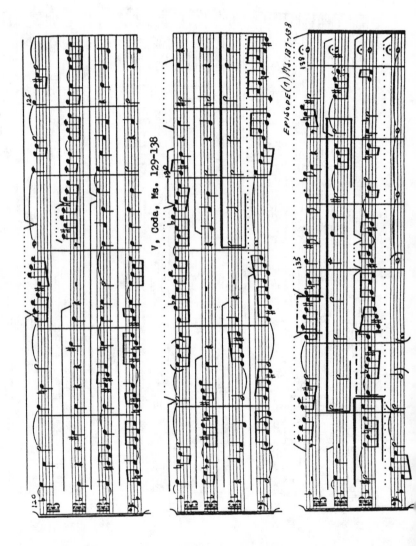

V, Coda, Ms. 129-138

EPISODE (1) Ms. 137-138

122

CONTRAPUNCTUS V
(a4) Ms. 1-90

I, Ms. 1-17

Exposition, Ms. 1-17

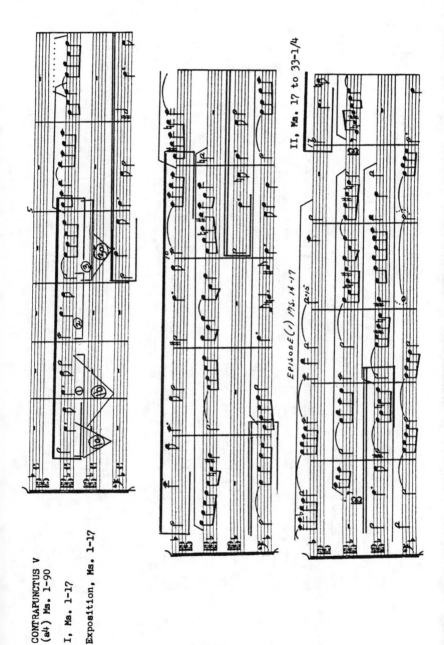

EPISODE (r) Ms. 14-17

II, Ms. 17 to 33-1/4

123

EPISODE (2) Ms. 30-33 1/4

IIIA, Ms. 33-41

124

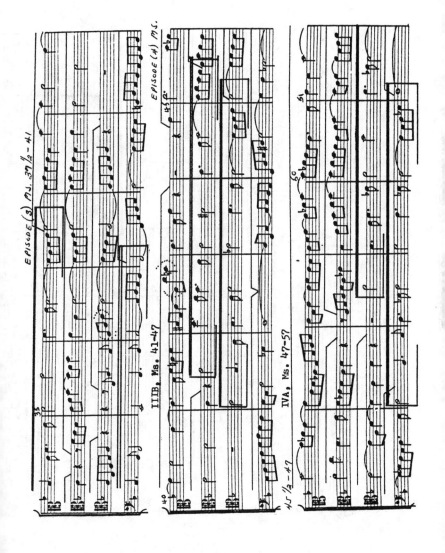

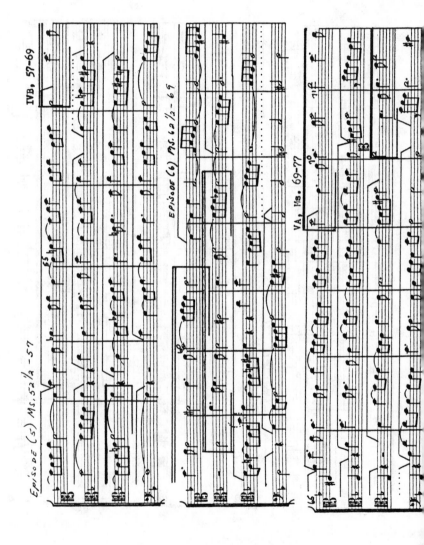

126

VI, Coda, Ms. 86-90.

127

CONTRAPUNCTUS VI
(a4) Ms. 1-79
DIVISION ONE
I, Exposition for
Subject, Ms. 1-9

III, Ms. 15 to 20-1/4

IV, Ms. 20-1/2 to 31; EPISODE (3) M.20-1/4

EPISODE (4) M.24-31/4

129

EPISODE (5) MS. 29-31

V, Ms. 31-35

DIVISION TWO, I, Ms. 35-47, Exposition for Answer

II, Ms. 47-57

131

132

IV, Ms. 63-1/2 to 74-1/2

133

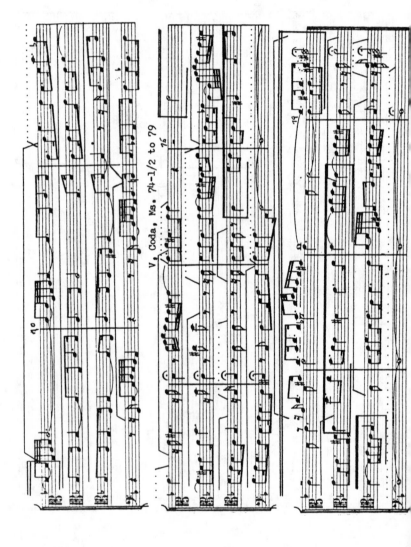

V, Coda, Ms. 74-1/2 to 79

CONTRAPUNCTUS VII
(a4) Ms. 1-61

I, Exposition,
Ms. 1 to 13-1/2

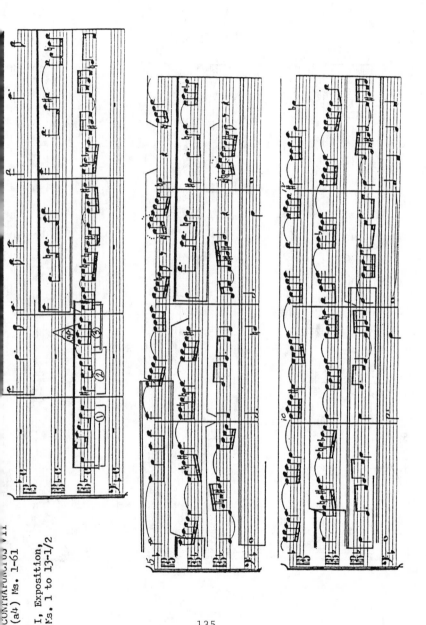

II, Ms. 13-1/2 to 20

EPISODE (1) Ms. 19-20 III, Ms. 20-35

136

137

EPISODE (2) Ms. 31½ - 35

IV, Ms. 35-45

138

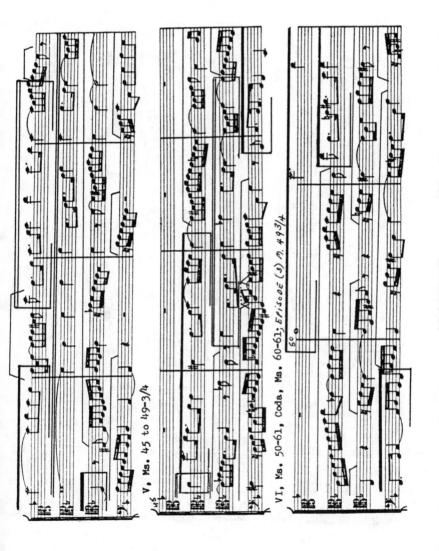

V, Ms. 45 to 49-3/4

VI, Ms. 50-61, Coda, Ms. 60-61, *EPISODE (3) m. #93/+*

139

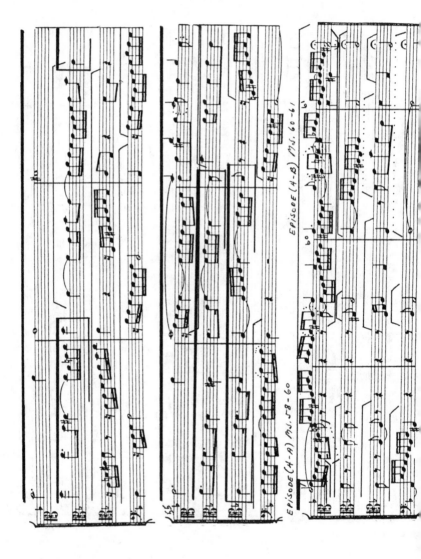

EPISODE (4-A) M.M. ♩=60

EPISODE (4-B) M.M. 60-61

140

Basic Fugue Subject
anticipating Sub. III

CONTRAPUNCTUS VIII
(a3) Ms. 1-188

DIVISION ONE, 1-39½
I, Exposition I,
Ms. 1-17

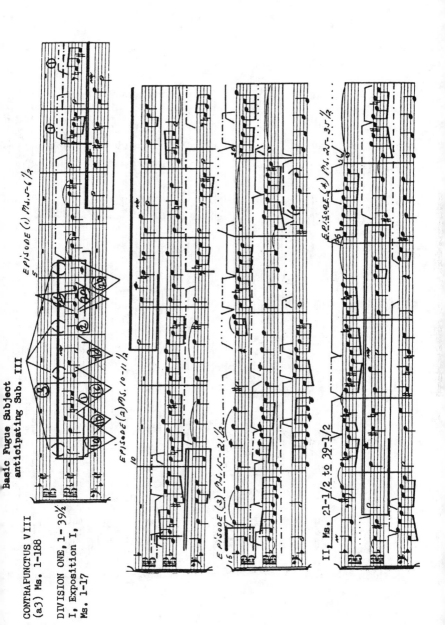

141

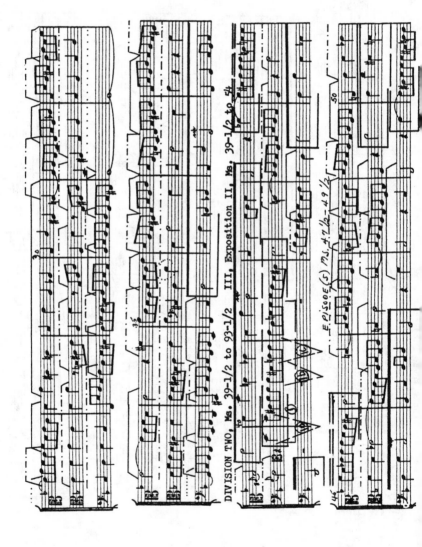

DIVISION TWO, Ms. 39-1/2 to 93-1/2   III, Exposition II, Ms. 39-1/2 to 54

Episode (s) Ms. 47 1/2 - 49 1/2

142

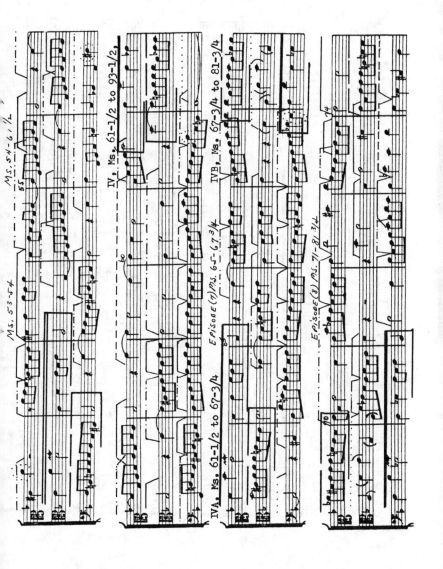

143

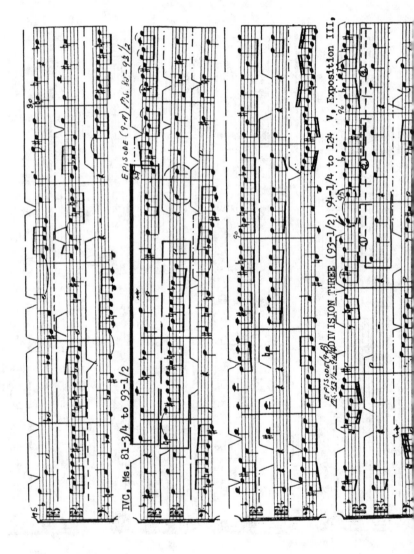

IVG, Ms. 81-3/4 to 93-1/2

EPISODE (9-A) Ms. 86 - 93 1/2

EPISODE (9-B)
Ms. 93 1/2 - 94 DIVISION THREE (93-1/2). 94-1/4 to 124 V, Exposition III,

145

146

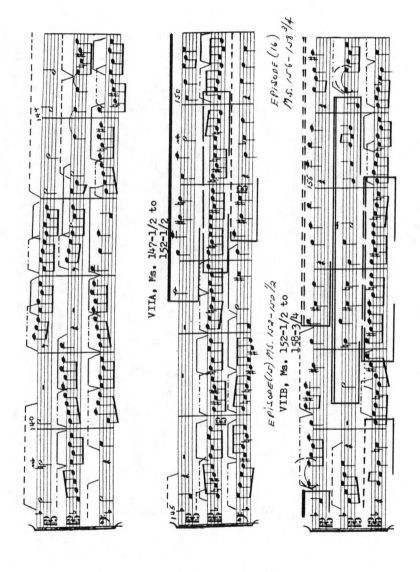

VIIA, Ms. 147-1/2 to 152-1/2

Episode (15) Ms. 152-152½
VIIB, Ms. 152-1/2 to 158-3/4

Episode (16)
Ms. 156-158 3/4

147

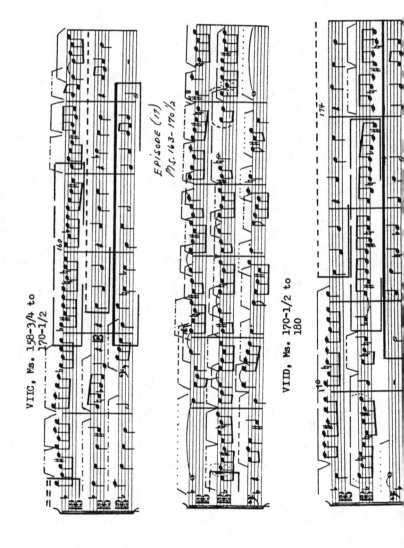

VIIC, Ms. 158-3/4 to 170-1/2

EPISODE (17)
Ms. 163-170 1/2

VIID, Ms. 170-1/2 to 180

148

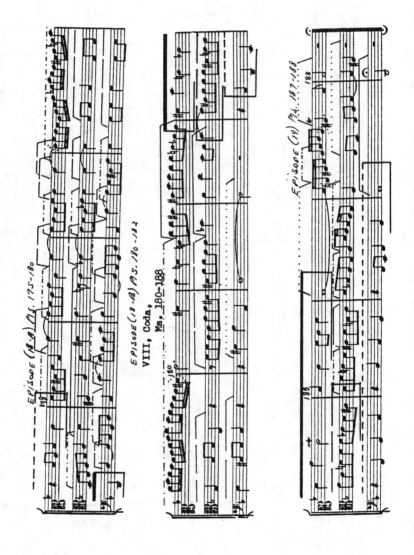

VIII, Coda,
Ms. 180—188

CONTRAPUNCTUS IX
(a4) Ms. 1-130

I, Ms. 1-35
Exposition,
Ms. 1-29

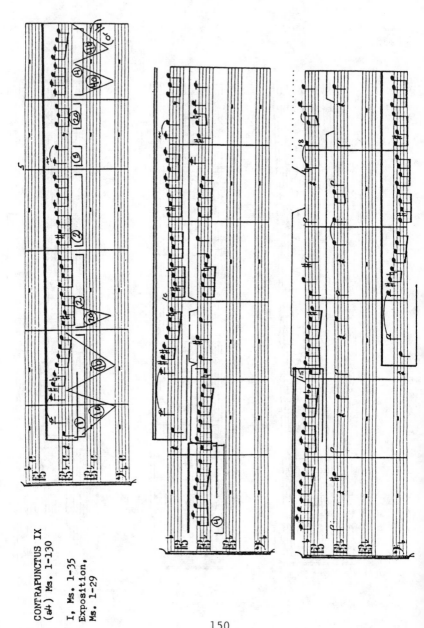

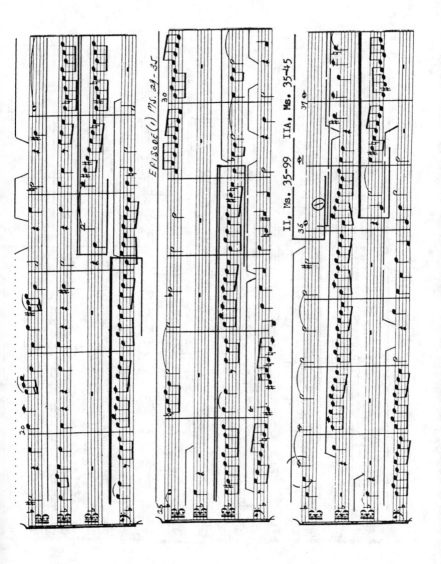

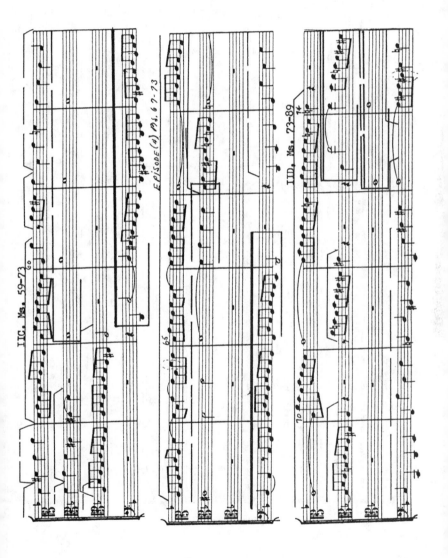

IIC, Ms. 59-73

EPISODE (4) Ms. 67-73

IID, Ms. 73-89

153

EPISODE(s) Mj.81-89

IIE, Ms. 89-99

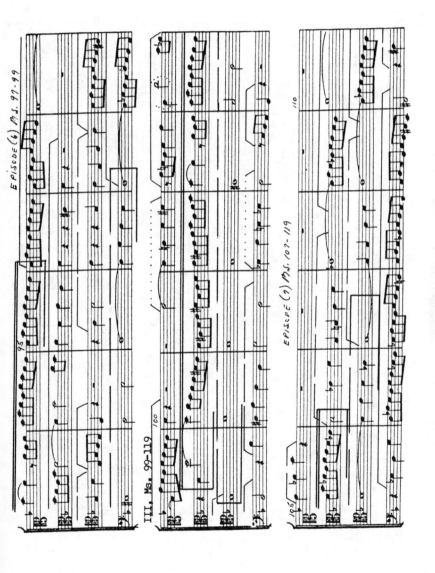

155

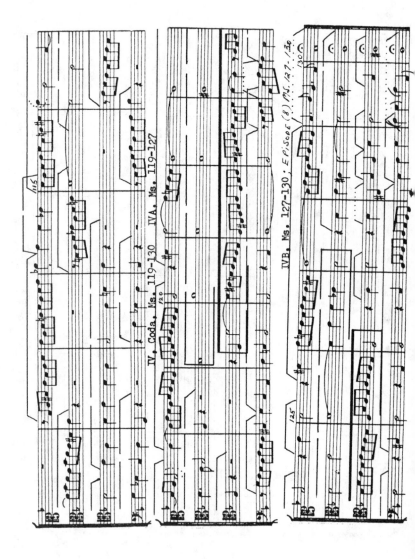

IV, Coda, Ms. 119-130   IVA, Ms. 119-127

IVB, Ms. 127-130 · Episode (8) Ms. 127-130

CONTRAPUNCTUS X
(a4) Ms. 1-120

DIVISION ONE,
Ms. 1(1/4) to 14-1/4

I, Exposition I,
Ms. 1(1/4) to 12

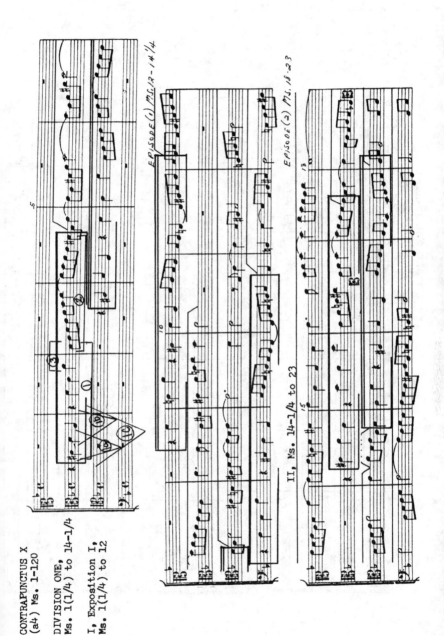

EPISODE (1) MS. 12-14 1/4

II, Ms. 14-1/4 to 23

EPISODE (2) MS. 18-23

157

DIVISION TWO, Ms. 23-44
III, Exposition II,

159

160

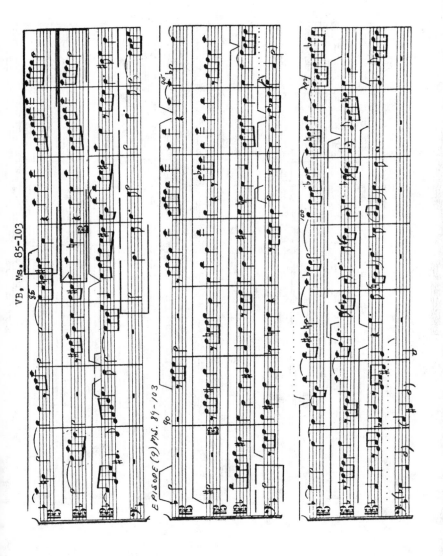

VB, Ms. 85-103

EPISODE (9) Ms. 89-103

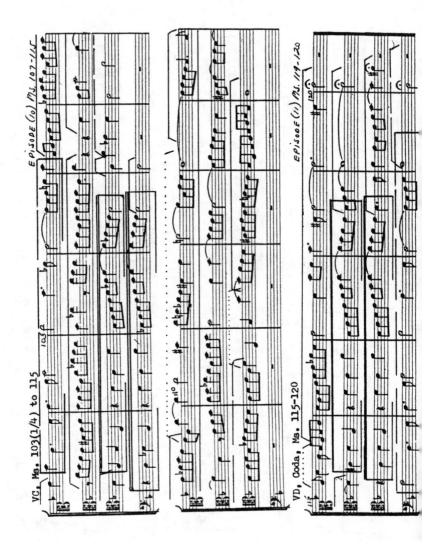

CONTRAPUNCTUS XI
(a4), Ms. 1-184

DIVISION ONE,
Ms. 1 to 27-1/2

I, Ms. 1-22

Exposition I,
Ms. 1-18

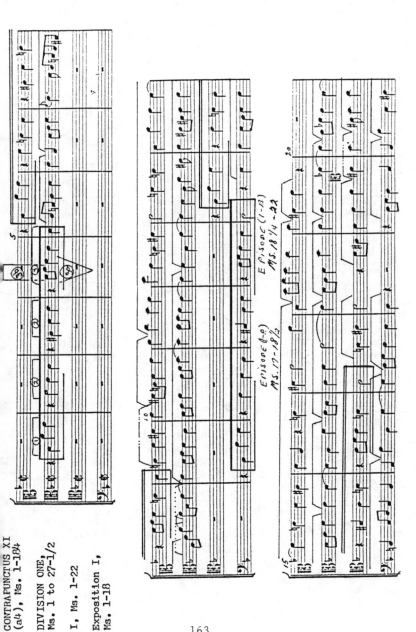

Episode (1-9)
Ms. 17-18½

Episode (1-13)
Ms. 18¼-22

163

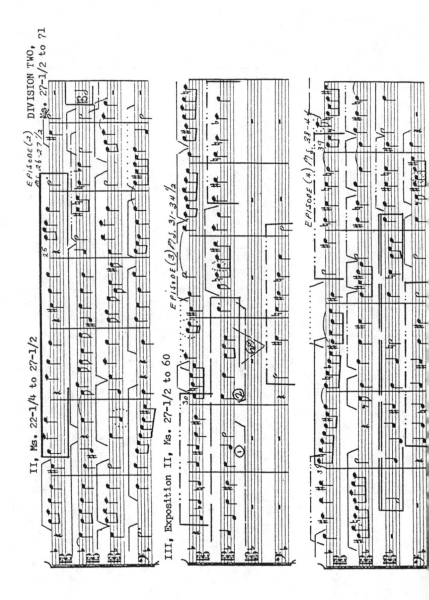

II, Ms. 22-1/4 to 27-1/2

Episode (2) *Ms. 26-27½* DIVISION TWO, Ms. 27-1/2 to 71

III, Exposition II, Ms. 27-1/2 to 60

Episode (3) Ms. 31-34½

Episode (4) Ms. 38-44

164

165

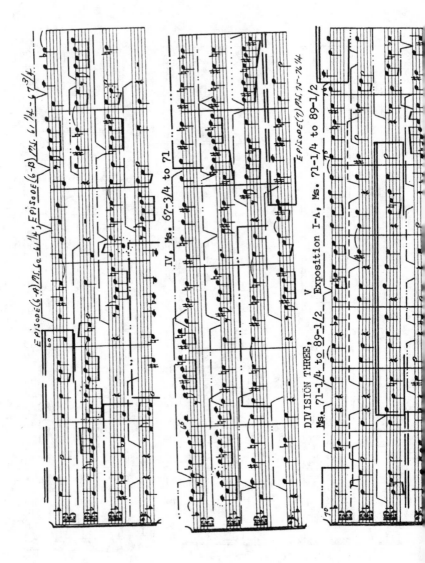

EPISODE (6-A) Ms. 60-1/4; EPISODE (6-B) Ms. 61-1/4 - 67-3/4.

IV, Ms. 67-3/4 to 71

EPISODE (7) Ms. 71-76-1/4

DIVISION THREE,
V
Ms. 71-1/4 to 89-1/2, Exposition I-A, Ms. 71-1/4 to 89-1/2

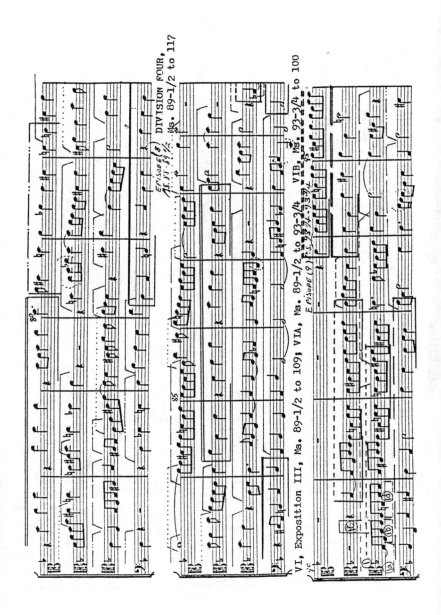

VI, Exposition III, Ms. 89-1/2 to 109; VIA, Ms. 89-1/2 to 92-3/4 VIB, Ms. 93-3/4 to 100

DIVISION FOUR, Ms. 89-1/2 to 117

Episode (8) Ms. 89-1/2

Episode (9) Ms. 93-3/4 to 93-3/4

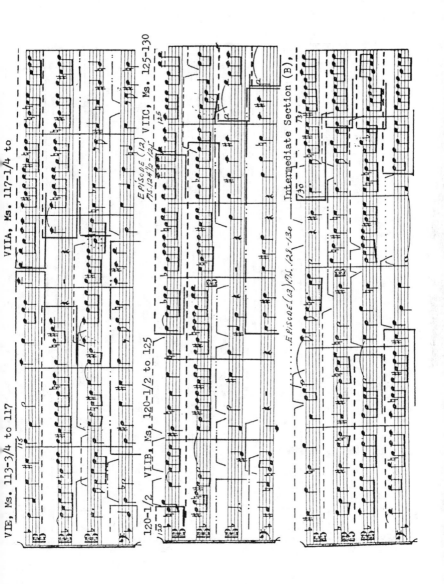

VIB, Ms. 113-3/4 to 117

VIIA, Ms. 117-1/4 to

VIIB, Ms. 120-1/2 to 125

120-1/2

EPISODE (1a) VIIC, Ms. 125-130
Ms. 124 1/2 - 125

EPISODE (1b) Ms. 125-130

Intermediate Section (B),

Ms. 130-1/4 to 132-1/2
VIII, Ms. 132-1/4 to 136-3/4

Episode (1/4)
Ms. 136—

136 3/4

135

IX, Ms. 136-3/4 to 140

Intermediate Section (C), Ms. 140-1/4 to 146

Episode (1/5)
Ms. 145—

X, Ms. 145-3/4 to 152-3/4

170

XIA, Ms. 152-3/4 to 158

XIB, Ms. 158-1/4 to 164-1/4

XIC, Ms. 164-1/4 to 168

Intermediate Section
(D), Ms. 167-3/4 to 175

171

XII, Coda, Ms. 174-3/4 to 184; XIIA, Ms. 174-3/4 to 179

XIIB, Ms. 179-3/4 to 184

CONTRAPUNCTUS XII

Canon alla Ottava

(Subject, Ms. 1-5)

(Answer, Ms. 5-9)

(Subject, Ms. 25-29)

(Answer, Ms. 29-33)

174

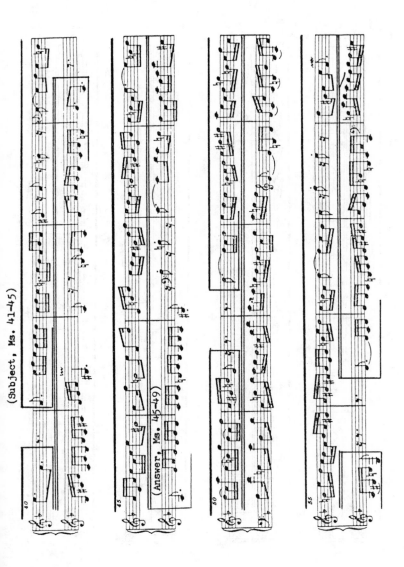
(Subject, Ms. 41–45)

(Answer, Ms. 45–49)

175

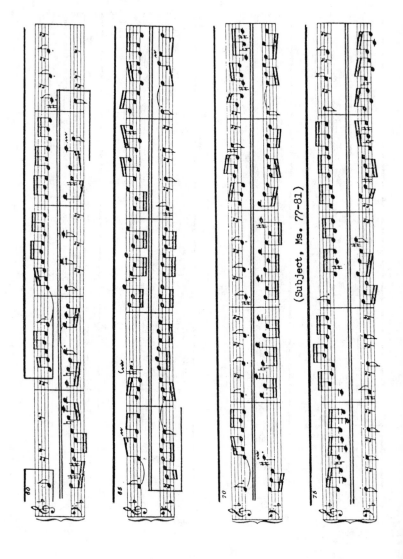

(Subject, Ms. 77-81)

176

(Answer, Ms. 81-85)

177

CONTRAPUNCTUS XIII

Canon alla Duodecima, in Contrapuncto alla Quinta

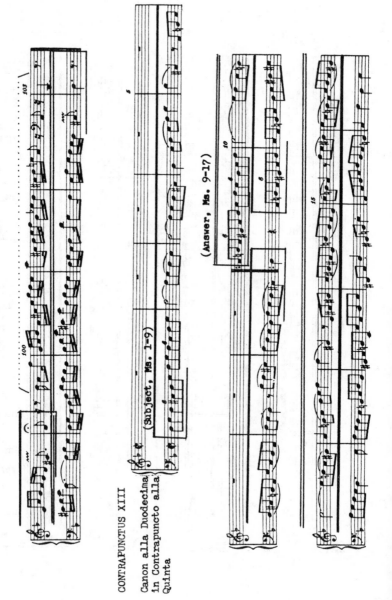

(Subject, Ms. 1-9)

(Answer, Ms. 9-17)

(Subject, ms. 34–42)

179

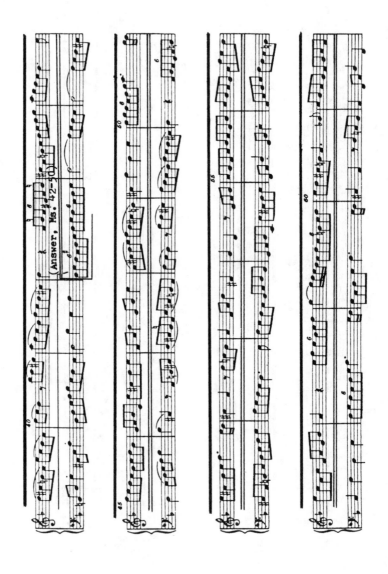

180

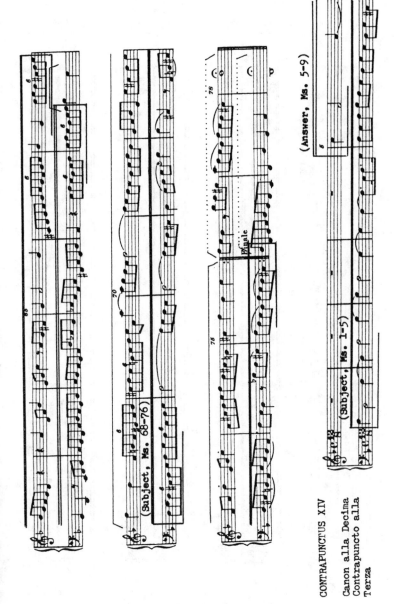

CONTRAPUNCTUS XIV

Canon alla Decima.
Contrapuncto alla
Terza

(Subject, Ms. 1-5)

(Answer, Ms. 5-9)

181

(Subject, Ms. 9-13)

(Answer, Ms. 13-17)

182

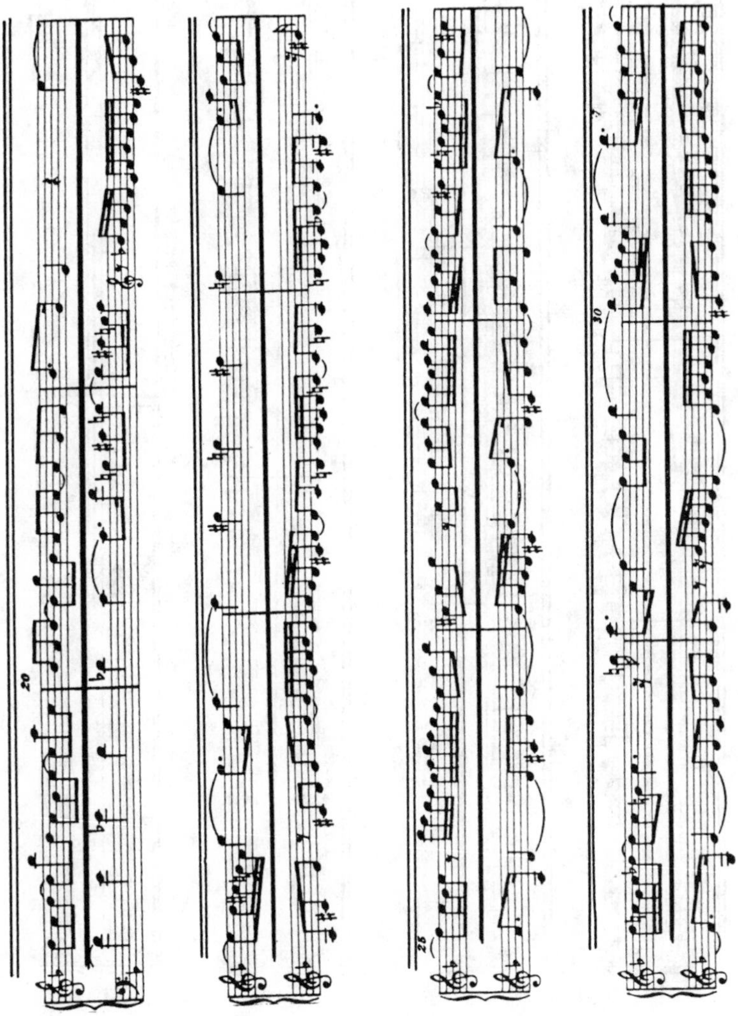

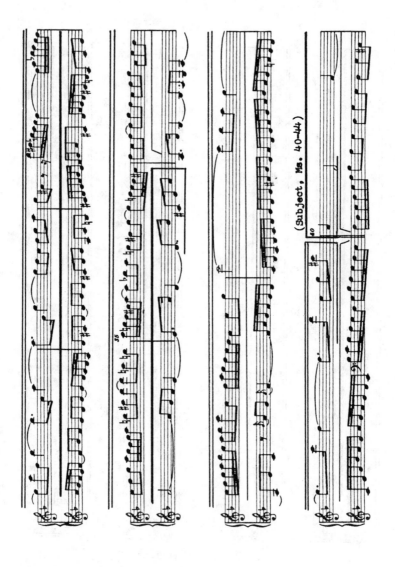

(Subject, Ms. 40-44)

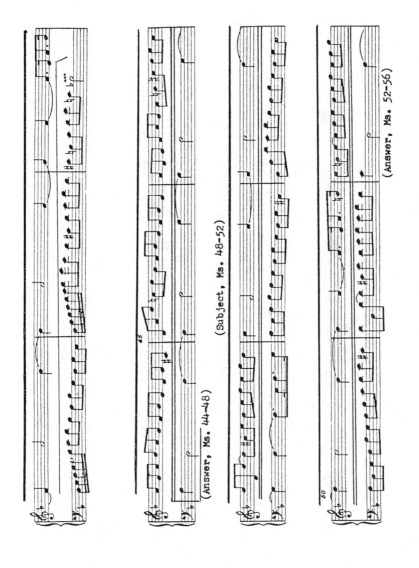

(Answer, Ms. 44-48)

(Subject, Ms. 48-52)

(Answer, Ms. 52-56)

185

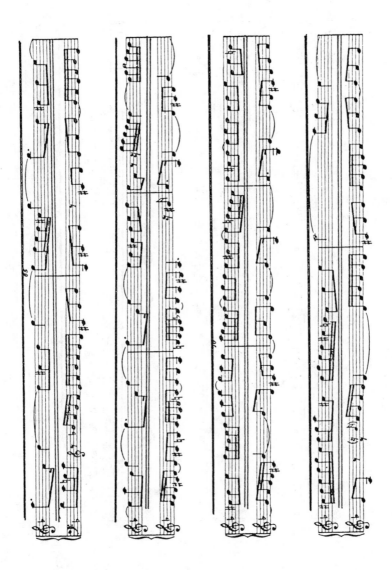

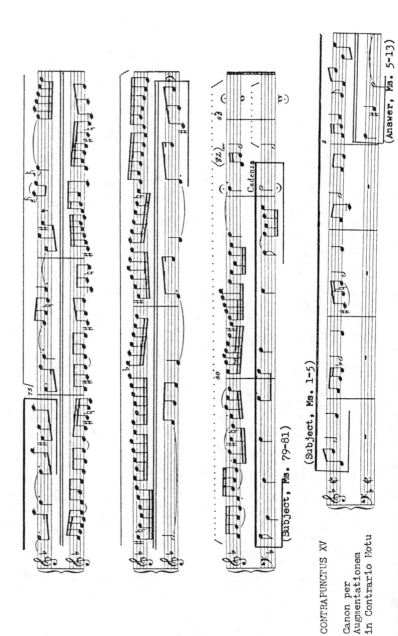

(Subject, Ms. 79-81)

(Subject, Ms. 1-5)

CONTRAPUNCTUS XV

Canon per
Augmentationem
in Contrario Motu

(Answer, Ms. 5-13)

188

189

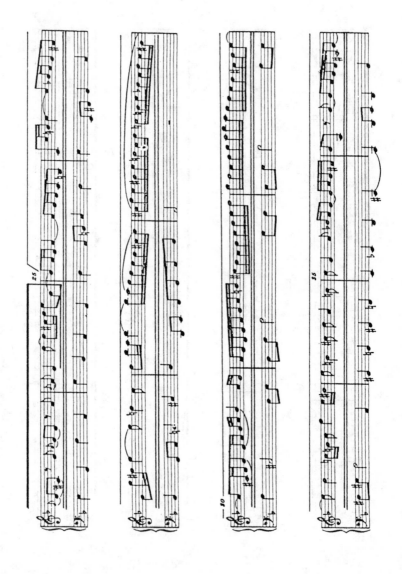

190

191

(Subject, Ms. 53-57)

(Answer, Ms. 57-65)

192

193

194

(Subject, Ms. 105-109)

195

CONTRAPUNCTUS XVI
(a3) Ms. 1-71
I, Ms. 1-20

Exposition, Ms. 1-13

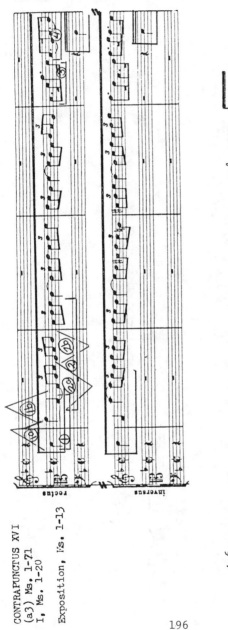

EPISODE (1) M.S. 13-20

197

II, Ms. 20-29

EPISODE (2) Ms. 24-29

198

III, Ms. 29-48

199

EPISODE (3) Ms. 41-48

200

IV, Ms. 48-62

EPISODE (4) Ms. 52-62

201

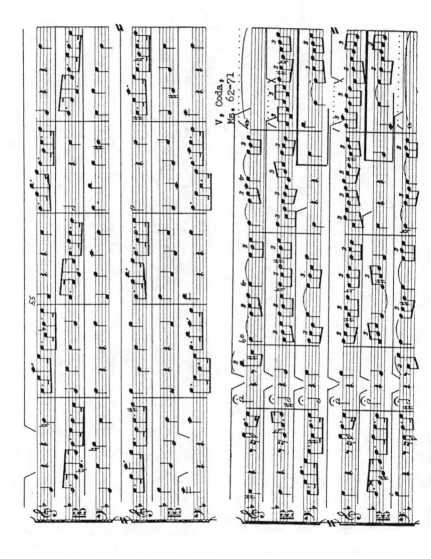

V, Coda,
Ms. 62-71

CONTRAPUNCTUS XVII
(a4) Ms. 1-56

I, Exposition,
Ms. 1-21

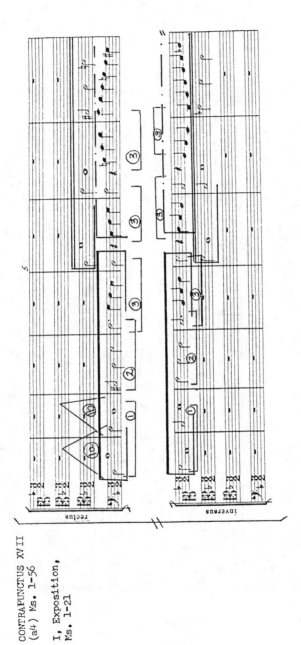

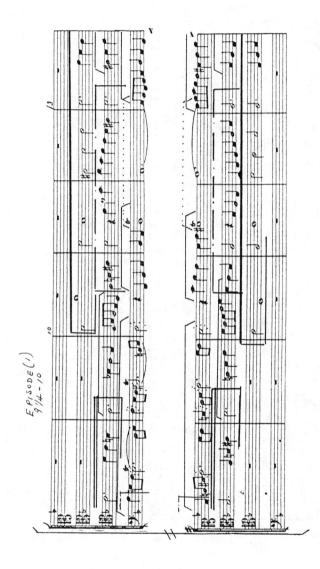

EPISODE (1)
9:14-10

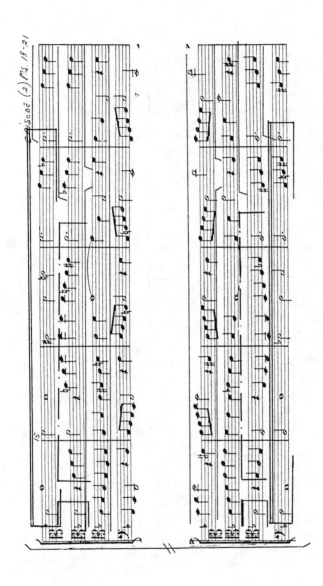

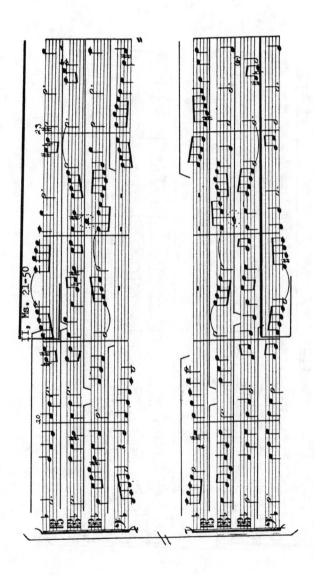

II, Ms. 21-50

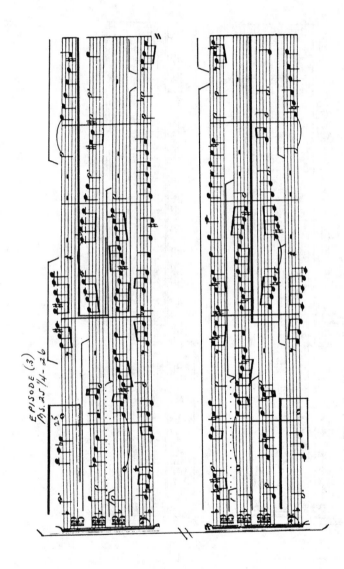

EPISODE (3)
Bs. 25/4-26

208

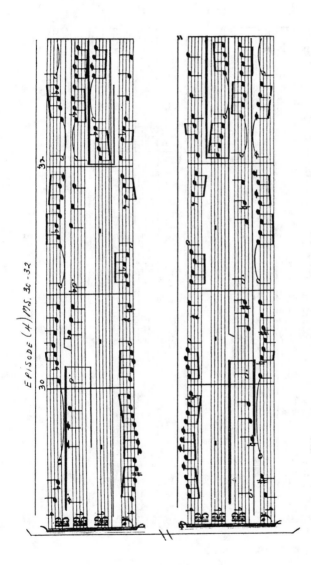

EPISODE (4) ms. 30 - 32

209

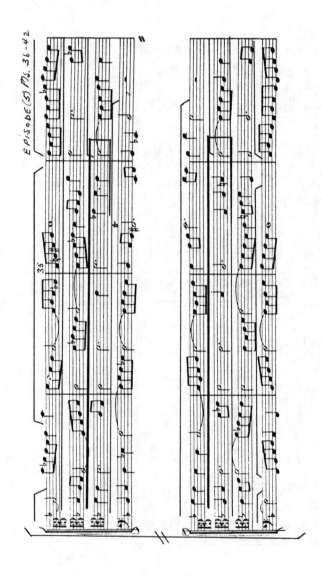

EPISODE(S) Ms. 36-42

210

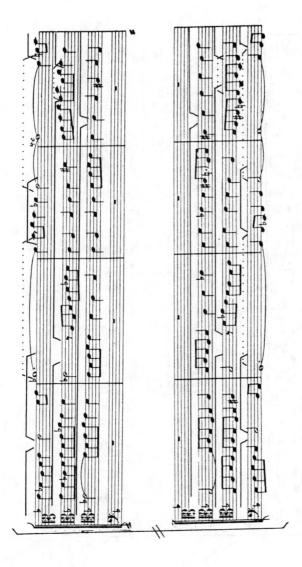

211

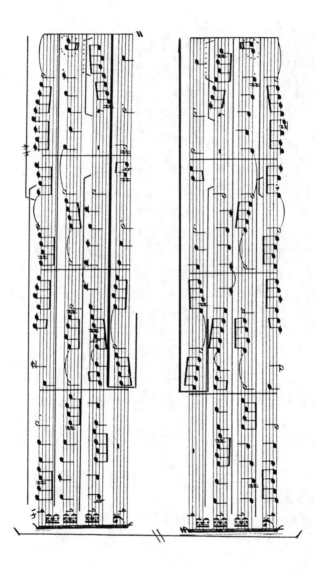

212

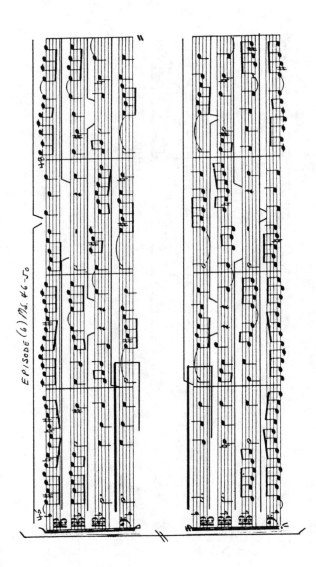

EPISODE (6) Ms. #6-50

213

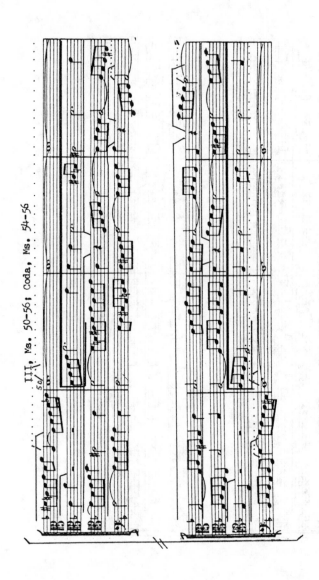

III, Ms. 50-56; Coda, Ms. 54-56

214

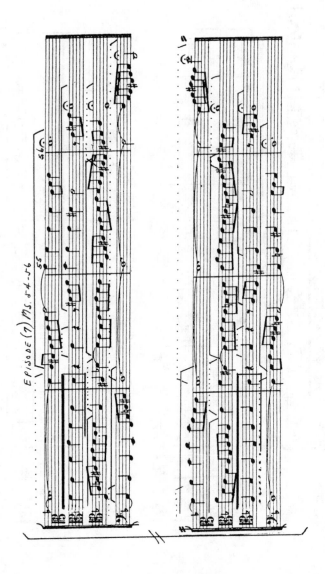

CONTRAPUNCTUS XVIII
(a4) Ms. 1-239

DIVISION ONE, Ms.
1-115

I, Exposition I,
Ms. 1 to 21-1/2

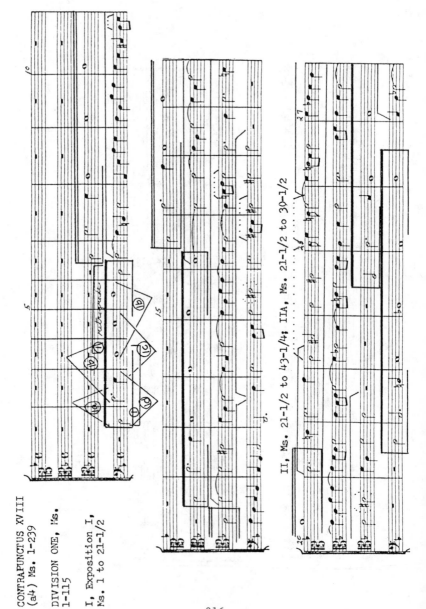

II, Ms. 21-1/2 to 43-1/4; IIA, Ms. 21-1/2 to 30-1/2

216

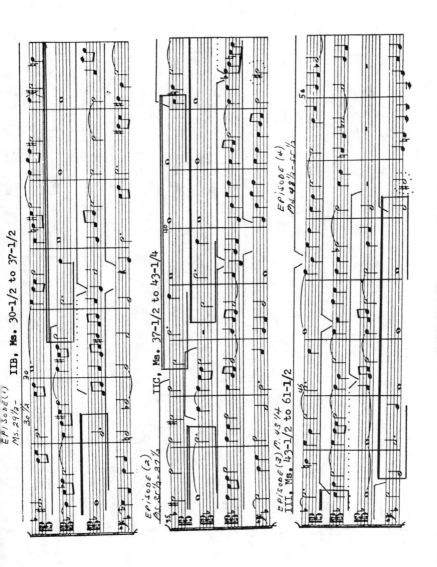

EPISODE (1)
Ms. 29½ –
IIB, Ms. 30-1/2 to 37-1/2

EPISODE (2)
Ms. 37½ – 37½
IIC, Ms. 37-1/2 to 43-1/4

EPISODE (3) M. 43 ¼
III, Ms. 43-1/2 to 61-1/2

EPISODE (4)
Ms. 43½ – 55 ½

217

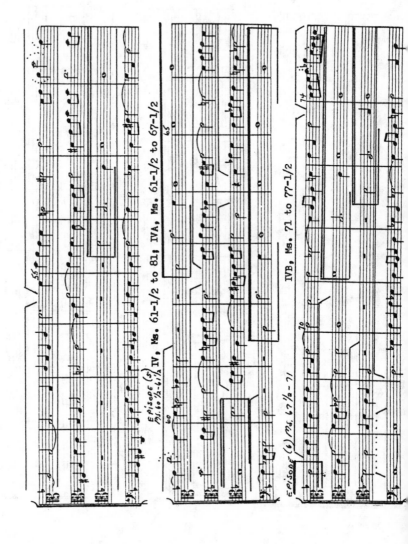

Episode (5)
Ms. 60½-67½; IV, Ms. 61-1/2 to 81; IVA, Ms. 61-1/2 to 67-1/2

IVB, Ms. 71 to 77-1/2

Episode (6) Ms. 67½-71

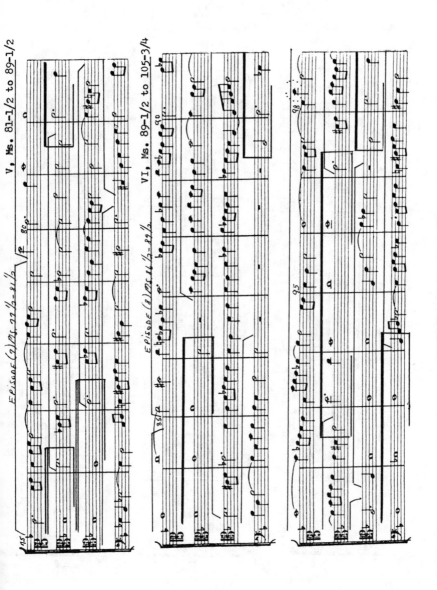

V, Ms. 81-1/2 to 89-1/2

VI, Ms. 89-1/2 to 105-3/4

219

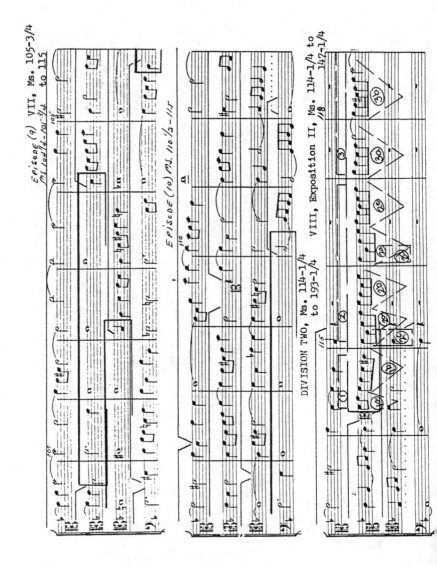

EPISODE (9) VII, Ms. 105-3/4 to 115
Ms. 104-1/4 - 104-3/4

EPISODE (10) Ms. 110-1/2 - 115

DIVISION TWO, Ms. 114-1/4 to 193-1/4

VIII, Exposition II, Ms. 114-1/4 to 142-1/4

EPISODE (12)
Ms. 141 1/4 - 147 1/4

IX, Ms. 147-1/4 to 180-1/4; IXA,

Ms. 147-1/4 to 156-1/4

EPISODE (13)
Ms. 147-1/4 - 156 1/4

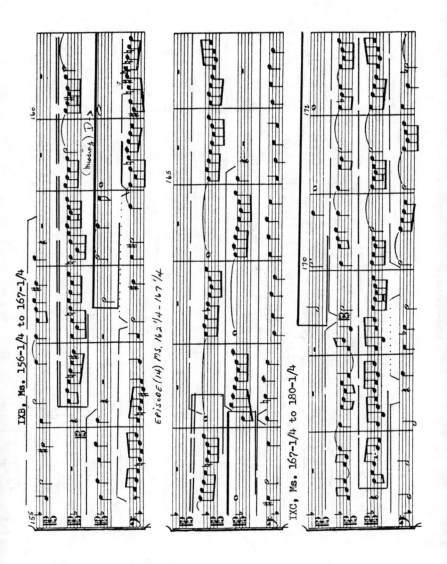

IXB, Ms. 156-1/4 to 167-1/4

EPISODE (1/4) MS. 162 1/4 - 167 1/4

IXC, Ms. 167-1/4 to 180-1/4

223

X, Ms. 180-1/4 to 193-1/4

224

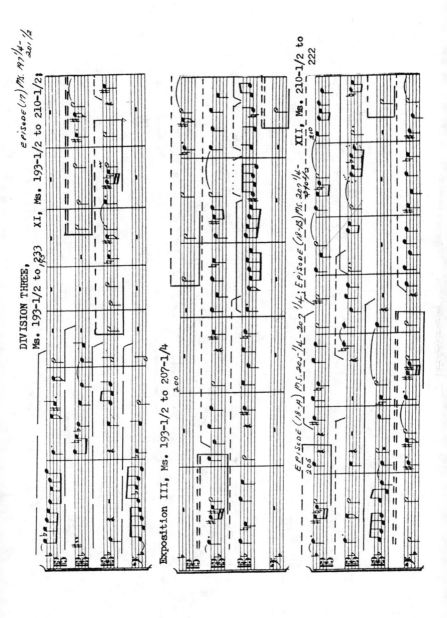

DIVISION THREE,

Ms. 193-1/2 to 233   XI, Ms. 193-1/2 to 210-1/2;   *Episode (17) Ms. 197 1/4 - 201, 1/2*

Exposition III, Ms. 193-1/2 to 207-1/4

Episode (18-A) Ms. 201-1/4-207 1/4; Episode (18-B) Ms. 207 1/4 - 210-1/2;   XII, Ms. 210-1/2 to 222

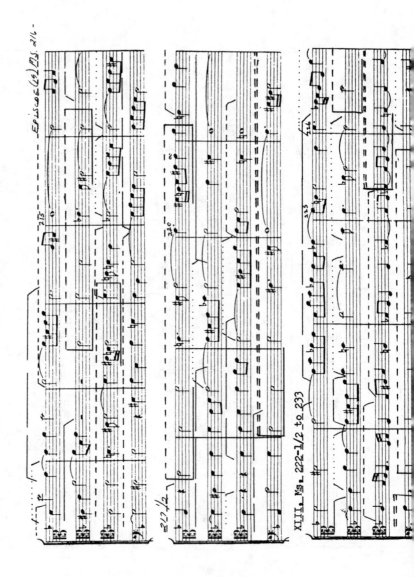

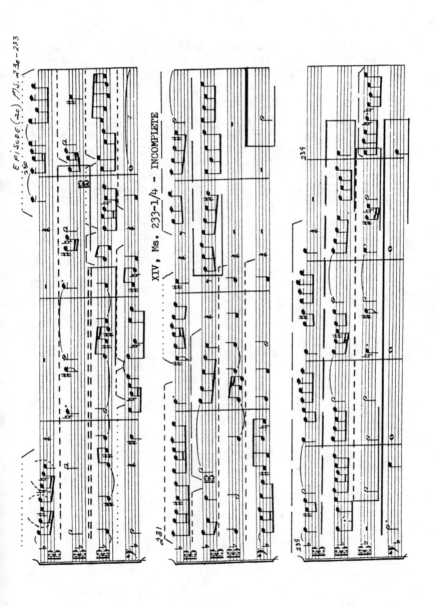

XIV, Ms. 233-1/4 - INCOMPLETE

227

THE SUBJECTS, EXPOSITIONS, AND COUNTER-SUBJECTS

THE SUBJECTS:

The subject has the potential to embody the style character[1], texture, and basis for motivic development in the entire fugue. The construction of each of these variants of the original subject influences the ultimate completed fugue.

The following tabulation of the subjects used in this work reveal that no two subjects are exactly the same for all twenty fugues. Rhythmic emphases, as found in stretto fugue Contrapunctus VI or mirror fugue Contrapunctus XVI, could have been incorporated in any of the simple fugues or double and triple fugues.

THE ORIGINAL SUBJECT

CONTRAPUNCTUS I, Simple Fugue

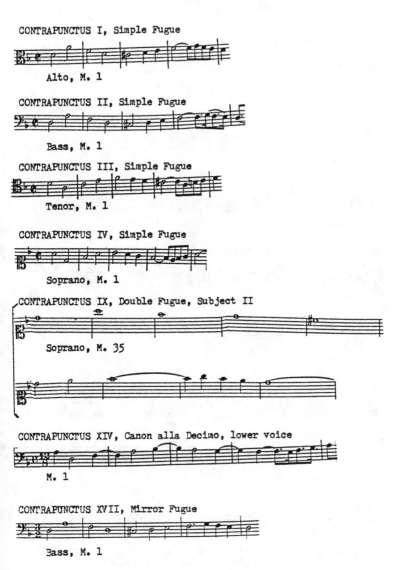

Alto, M. 1

CONTRAPUNCTUS II, Simple Fugue

Bass, M. 1

CONTRAPUNCTUS III, Simple Fugue

Tenor, M. 1

CONTRAPUNCTUS IV, Simple Fugue

Soprano, M. 1

CONTRAPUNCTUS IX, Double Fugue, Subject II

Soprano, M. 35

CONTRAPUNCTUS XIV, Canon alla Decimo, lower voice

M. 1

CONTRAPUNCTUS XVII, Mirror Fugue

Bass, M. 1

CONTRAPUNCTUS V, Stretto Fugue

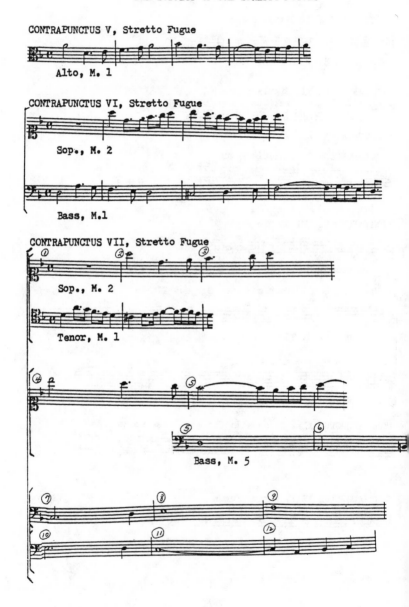

Alto, M. 1

CONTRAPUNCTUS VI, Stretto Fugue

Sop., M. 2

Bass, M.1

CONTRAPUNCTUS VII, Stretto Fugue

Sop., M. 2

Tenor, M. 1

Bass, M. 5

230

(THE SUBJECT OF THE STRETTO FUGUES, continued.)

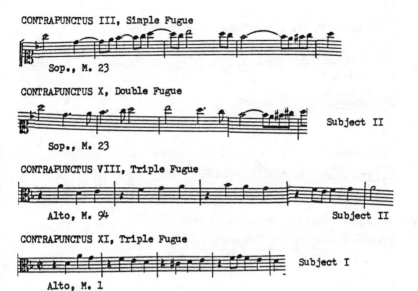

CONTRAPUNCTUS III, Simple Fugue

Sop., M. 23

CONTRAPUNCTUS X, Double Fugue

Sop., M. 23

Subject II

CONTRAPUNCTUS VIII, Triple Fugue

Alto, M. 94

Subject II

CONTRAPUNCTUS XI, Triple Fugue

Subject I

Alto, M. 1

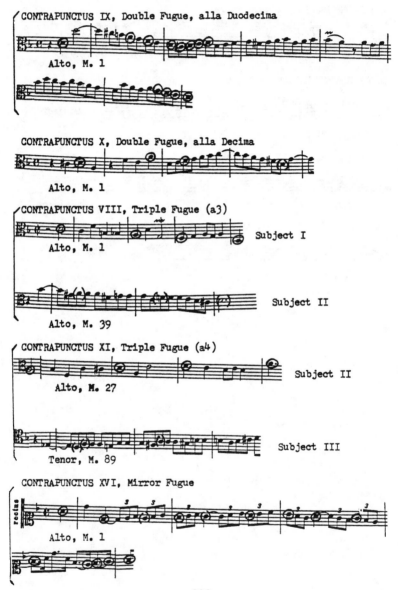

CONTRAPUNCTUS IX, Double Fugue, alla Duodecima

Alto, M. 1

CONTRAPUNCTUS X, Double Fugue, alla Decima

Alto, M. 1

CONTRAPUNCTUS VIII, Triple Fugue (a3)

Alto, M. 1 — Subject I

Alto, M. 39 — Subject II

CONTRAPUNCTUS XI, Triple Fugue (a4)

Alto, M. 27 — Subject II

Tenor, M. 89 — Subject III

CONTRAPUNCTUS XVI, Mirror Fugue

Alto, M. 1

(NEW AND EXTENDED SUBJECTS, continued)

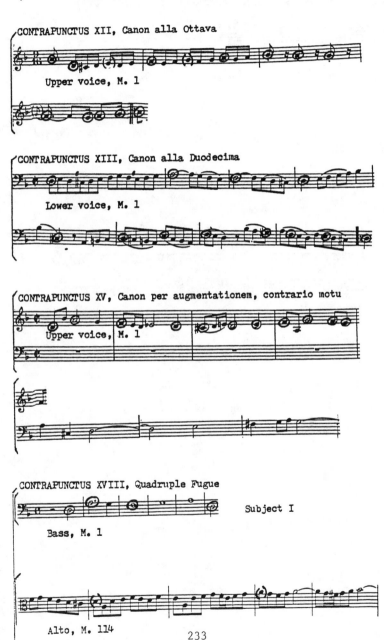

CONTRAPUNCTUS XII, Canon alla Ottava

Upper voice, M. 1

CONTRAPUNCTUS XIII, Canon alla Duodecima

Lower voice, M. 1

CONTRAPUNCTUS XV, Canon per augmentationem, contrario motu

Upper voice, M. 1

CONTRAPUNCTUS XVIII, Quadruple Fugue

Subject I

Bass, M. 1

Alto, M. 114

(NEW AND EXTENDED SUBJECTS, continued)

 Subject II

NEW SUBJECT, NOT BASED ON THE ORIGINAL FUGUE SUBJECT,
THE B-A-C-H THEME

 Subject III

Tenor, M. 193

234

THE EXPOSITIONS:

The function of each exposition is to present the basic ideas present in each respective fugue. In addition to varying the entrances of voices and the order of the subject, each of the expositions presents a new procedure for its completion.

The special usage of pedal point in simple fugue Contrapunctus II could be added to any fugue type. The carefully-planned episodes within the expositions could vary with the latent intent of the overall fugue structure, but not be limited by fugue types.

The inclusion of the subject in both normal and inverted orders can be symmetrically a part of any fugue type. While Bach does not illustrate this additional procedure, the method of answering the subjects in the stretto fugues by notes in diminution or augmentation could conceivably be used for contrapuntal contrast in fugue types other than the stretto fugues.

A double exposition procedure as implied in stretto fugues Contrapunctus V and VI could be useful for any fugue type. The extent to which a subject can be presented in an exposition bordering on a separate fughetta can vary with any fugue type. Contrasting expositions in double, triple, or quadruple fugues can have an infinite list of complementary ideas.

In the author's article entitled "A Collation of the Expositions in DIE KUNST DER FUGE of J.S. Bach (Bach, The Quarterly Journal of the Riemenschneider Bach Institute, Volume XII, No. 2, April, 1981, p. 28), a chart was made tabulating the order of entry of the various voices in the expositions. From such a tabulation, an interesting idea for consideration begins to surface when the ultimate length of DIE KUNST DER FUGE is discussed. The scheme of entries for the four simple fugues is the only fugue type that includes four different examples, each of which begins with a new voice. Perhaps Bach planned to include four different examples of each fugue type, illustrating changes necessary when the entrance voice is varied. Especially does this seem possible when so many of Bach's fugues begin with the alto voice, as does the first contrapunctus of this work.

THE EXPOSITIONS

CONTRAPUNCTUS	ANSWER	COUNTER-SUBJECT	EPISODES BETWEEN SUBJECTS AND ANSWERS	EPISODE AT END OF EXPOSITIONS	CADENCE AT END OF EXPOSITIONS	STRETTO STATEMENTS IN EXPOSITIONS	OTHER DISTINCTIVE ATTRIBUTES
THE FOUR SIMPLE FUGUES							
I Ms. 1-17	Tonal	Tonal CS in Expo. only	None	None	Plagal in D Minor	None	
II Ms. 1-23	Tonal	Free, or "migrating"	None	5 Ms. with pedal points and cadentially ornamented melodic line	Dominant of D Minor	None	Rhythmic interest included in the original subject
III Ms. 1-19	Tonal	Basically real	One, 2 Ms. between 3rd and 4th statements	None	Dominant of D Minor	None	Chromatic CS creates harmonic intensity
IV Ms. 1-19	Tonal	Tonal, with frequent paired voices in imitation	One, 2 Ms. between 2nd and 3rd statements	None	D Minor	None	CS and Free Material independent, including descending 3rd motive; order of entry of voices in Expo. guide to remaining voices entrances
THE THREE STRETTO FUGUES							
V, Expo. I, Ms. 1-17, stating Sub. and Ans. in normal and inverted orders	Tonal	Free	None	3 Ms.	Dominant of D Minor	Each new statement enters after 3 Ms.	Subject of stretto fugues is variant of original subject; normal note values

236

THE EXPOSITIONS (continued)

CONTRAPUNCTUS	ANSWER	COUNTER-SUBJECT	EPISODES BE-TWEEN SUBJECTS AND ANSWERS	EPISODE AT END OF EXPO-SITIONS	CADENCE AT END OF EXPOSITIONS	STRETTO STATEMENTS IN EXPOSITIONS	OTHER DISTINCTIVE ATTRIBUTES
(V), Expo. II, Ms. 17-33-1/4 Sub. inverted, Ans. normal	Tonal	Free	None	1 Ms.	Deceptive cadence in D Minor	Each new statement enters after 3 Ms.	Throughout fugue, order of statements in Expo. II followed (1)
VI, Expo. I in Div. One, Ms. 1-9(-12) emphasizes Subject (2)	Tonal	Free	One, 1-1/2 Ms. between 3rd and 4th statements	None, but includes pedal point	A Minor	Tightening of stretto	Normal and dim. note values; 6 circular statements: (Ms. 1-12) B S A T A S; rhythmic interest included in Subject
Expo. II in Div. Two, Ms. 35-47 emphasizes Answer	Tonal	Free	One, 2-1/2 Ms. between 3rd and 4th statements	4 Ms.	D Minor	Same as Expo. I	
VII, Ms. 1-13-1/2	Tonal	Free	None	None	D Major tri-ad as dom-inant of G Minor	Tightening of stretto	Normal, dim., and aug. note values; no triple stretto occurs in Expo.; combinations of voices reoccur later in fugue(3)

237

THE EXPOSITIONS (continued)

CONTRAPUNCTUS	ANSWER	COUNTER-SUBJECT	EPISODES BE-TWEEN SUBJECTS AND ANSWERS	EPISODE AT END OF EXPO-SITIONS	CADENCE AT END OF EXPOSITIONS	STRETTO STATEMENTS IN EXPOSITIONS	OTHER DISTINCTIVE ATTRIBUTES
THE TWO DOUBLE FUGUES							
IX, Expo. I, Ms. 1–29 new subject	Real	Free	None	None	D Minor	None	All entrances of Sub. I begin on 2nd beat of Measure
Expo. II, Ms. 35–99, original sub-ject in aug.	Tonal, alter-nates F Major and A Minor with Subject	Free (Sub. I)	Episodes sepa-rate each	1 Ms.	A Minor	Each statement in stretto with Sub. I	
X, Expo. I, in Div. One, Ms. 1–1/4 to 12, new subject	Tonal	Free	None	None	D Minor	Stretto after varying dis-tances	Complex rhythm and implied harmony in Sub. I for later development; each sub. presented in its own fughetta$_{(4)}$
Expo. II, in Div. Two, Ms. 23–38 stretto sub.	Tonal, G Minor and A Minor	Free	One, 1 Ms. between 2nd and 3rd statements	5 Ms.	D Minor	Stretto with false entry	Expo. ends with 3 voices; no two statements of Sub. I or Answer I are identical

THE EXPOSITIONS (continued)

CONTRAPUNCTUS	ANSWER	COUNTER-SUBJECT	EPISODES BETWEEN SUBJECTS AND ANSWERS	EPISODE AT END OF EXPOSITIONS	CADENCE AT END OF EXPOSITIONS	STRETTO STATEMENTS IN EXPOSITIONS	OTHER DISTINCTIVE ATTRIBUTES
THE TWO TRIPLE FUGUES							
VIII, Expo. I, in Div. One, Ms. 1-17, new subject	Real	Real, in Expo. only	Two, between each statement	6 Ms.	D Minor	None	Each subject presented in its own fughetta;(5) alto introduces all three subjects
Expo. II, in Div. Two, Ms. 39-1/2 to 54, new subject	Real	Sub. II partially a CS for Sub.	One, between 2nd and 3rd statements	8 Ms.	D Minor	All statements in stretto with Sub. I	
Expo. III, in Div. Three, 94-1/4 to 117-1/4 stretto sub., rhythmically altered	Tonal	Free	Two, between each statement	15 Ms.	D Minor	None	Expo. III has same order of entry of voices as Expo. I
XI, Expo. I(6), in Div. One, Ms. 1-18, stretto sub., rhythmically altered	Real	Free	None	1-1/2 Ms.	D Minor	None	
Expo. II in Div. Two, Ms. 27-1/2 to	Basically real	Freely treated "chroma-	Three lengthy episodes between each state-	1-1/2 Ms.	C Major	None	"Chromatic motive" with Sub. II gives to that Div.

239

THE EXPOSITIONS (continued)

CONTRAPUNCTUS	ANSWER	COUNTER-SUBJECT	EPISODES BE-TWEEN SUBJECTS AND ANSWERS	EPISODE AT END OF EXPO-SITIONS	CADENCE AT END OF EXPOSITIONS	STRETTO STATEMENTS IN EXPOSITIONS	OTHER DISTINCTIVE ATTRIBUTES
		tic motive"	ment				harmonic coloring
60, new subject							
Expo. IA,(7) in Div. Three, Ms. 71-1/4 to 89-1/2, Sub. I inverted	Tonal	Free	One, between 1st and 2nd statements	1-1/2 Ms.	F Major	None	Subject I has separate Expo. for both normal and inverted orders
Expo. III, in Div. Four, Ms. 89-1/2 to 109, new subject	Tonal	Free	Two	3 Ms.	B-flat Major	All statements in stretto with another subject	
THE TWO MIRROR FUGUES							
XVI, Ms. 1-13, new subject	Tonal	Free	None	None	A Minor, Rectus G Minor, Inv.	None	Intricate rhythmic combinations
XVII, Ms. 1-21, original subject, different meter	Tonal	Reference to a CS in Expo.	One, 1/2 Ms.	None	F Major, Rectus, (D Minor), D Minor, Inv.	None	Subject becomes elaborated in 3 versions; order of voices in Expo. followed throughout
THE QUADRUPLE FUGUE							
XVIII, Expo.	Tonal	Free	None	None	D Minor	None	Each of the 3 Sub-

THE EXPOSITIONS (continued)

CONTRAPUNCTUS	ANSWER	COUNTER-SUBJECT	EPISODES BE-TWEEN SUBJECTS AND ANSWERS	EPISODE AT END OF EXPO-SITIONS	CADENCE AT END OF EXPOSITIONS	STRETTO STATEMENTS IN EXPOSITIONS	OTHER DISTINCTIVE ATTRIBUTES
One, Ms. 1-21-1/2, new subject							fughetta
Expo. II, Div. Two, Ms. 114-1/4 to 147-1/4, new subject	Real	Free	One, 1 Ms. between 2nd - 3rd statements	None (7 ms.)	A Minor (D Minor)	None	
Expo. III, Div. Three, Ms. 193-1/2 to 207-1/4, B-A-C-H theme (8)	Real	Free	One, 2 Ms. between 2nd and 3rd state-ments	None (2 ms.)	A Minor	Two, 1 Ms. stretto statements	

241

FOOTNOTES FOR CHART OF EXPOSITIONS

(1) All four voices present a different version of the subject or answer in each exposition:

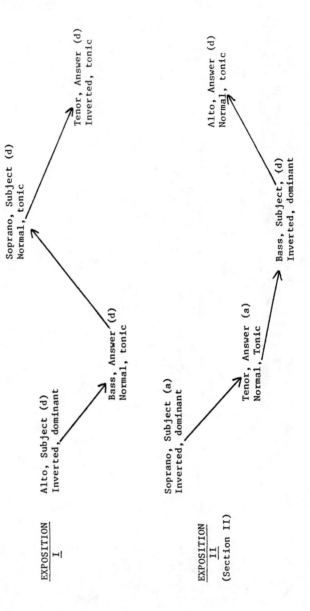

EXPOSITION
I

Alto, Subject (d)
Inverted, dominant

Bass, Answer (d)
Normal, tonic

Soprano, Subject (d)
Normal, tonic

Tenor, Answer (d)
Inverted, tonic

EXPOSITION
II
(Section II)

Soprano, Subject (a)
Inverted, dominant

Tenor, Answer (a)
Normal, Tonic

Bass, Subject, (d)
Inverted, dominant

Alto, Answer (d)
Normal, tonic

(2) A comparison of these two expositions shows these similarities:

I				II			
Ms. 1-5	B	S	normal	Ms. 35-39	S	A	inverted
Ms. 2-4	S	A	inverted, dim.	Ms. 36-38	B	S	normal, dim.
Ms. 3-1/2 to 5-1/2	A	S	normal, dim.	Ms. 37-1/2 to 39-1/2	T	A	inverted, dim.
Episode, 1-1/2 Ms.				Episode, 2-1/2 Ms.			
Ms. 7-9	T	A	inverted, dim.	Ms. 42-44	A	A	inverted, dim.

(3) Many procedures found in the exposition are used later in this fugue. The exposition begins and ends with the tenor, both statements in diminution: the first as subject in normal order, and the second as answer in inverted order. The idea of beginning and ending a section with the same voice is followed in Section IV.

In addition to the framework planning of the exposition, the voices combine in two significant ways. In Ms. 1-6, the soprano as answer inverted, in normal note values, is surrounded by subject in diminution, first normal, then inverted. Following these three voices, and with the entrance of the bass answer in augmentation in M. 5, the bass continues with two statements of the subject and answer in diminution. This grouping of two similar statements with the same note values with a third statement in contrasting note values occurs frequently in this fugue.

The exposition ends with the augmented statement heard by itself for several measures.. The last statement of the subject in augmentation stated by the soprano in Ms. 57-58 also ends by itself.

In the first four statements in the exposition, both subjects are in diminution, but in normal and inverted orders, while the answers are inverted, first with normal note values and then in augmentation. Following the first statement of the subject in M. 1, all versions are heard in this sequence:

M. 2	Answer	inverted	normal note values
M. 3	Subject	inverted	diminution
M. 5	Answer	inverted	augmentation

(4) The order of entry of voices in the two expositions is similar, the outer voices being interchanged, and the inner voices remaining the same:

Exposition I	Exposition II
A	S
T	(A) T
B	B
S	A

(5) A definitive cadence ending occurs in M. 39-1/2 directly preceding the start of Division Two. The sequence of voices for Subject I spans the ending in M. 39-1/2. Although the definitive cadence ends a complete Division of Subject I, the order of entrance of voices for Subject I continues from Division One into Division Two:

DIVISION ONE
Section I, Exposition I

Subject I	A
Answer I	B
Subject I	S

Section II

| Answer I | A |
| Subject I | B |

Start of
DIVISION TWO

| Subject I | S |

The last statement of Subject I in Division Two is combined with the first statement of Subject II.

No episode exists between the end of Division One and the start of Division Two. Attention is thus drawn to the combination of Subject I with a possible new counter-subject, which in reality is the new Subject II.

(6) The order of entry of voices in the three (four) expositions is:

Exposition I (Division One)	Exposition II (Division Two)	Exposition IA (Division Three)	Exposition III (Division Four)
A	A	T	T
S	T	S	S
B	B	B	B
T	S	A	A

Expositions IA and III have the same order of entry of voices.

(7) The order of entries of Expositions I and IA could be compared as follows:

Exposition I (Division One)

Subject I	A	normal	tonic	d
Answer I	S	normal	dominant	d
Subject I	B	normal	tonic	d
Answer I	T	normal	dominant	d

Exposition IA (Division Three)

Answer I	T	inverted	dominant	a
Answer I	S	inverted	dominant	d
Subject I	B	inverted	tonic	d
Answer I	A	inverted	dominant	d

The two outer voices are interchanged, with the two inner voices remaining the same, resulting in contrasting pairs of voices.

With the exception of the second Answer I by the soprano in Exposition IA, which is one measure following the preceding statement, the two expositions plan every new statement to enter on the beat following the preceding statement. The extra measure may have been added in Contrapunctus XI for four voices to draw attention to the similarity of structure between the last three voices in this Section V, and Section V in Contrapunctus VIII in three voices.

(8) The order of entry of the three subjects in their respective expositions is:

Exposition I		Exposition II		Exposition III	
Subject I	B	Subject II	A	Subject III	T
Answer I	T	Answer II	S	Answer III	A
Subject I	A	Subject II	B	Subject III	S
Answer I	S	Answer II	T	Answer III	B

Exposition I begins and ends with outer voices. Exposition II begins and ends with inner voices. Exposition III begins with an inner voice, and ends with an outer voice.

246

Contrapunctus II, Ms. 1-23

EPISODE(1) MS. 17-23

248

Contrapunctus III, Ms. 1-19

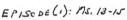

EPISODE (1): Ms. 13-15

Contrapunctus IV, Ms. 1-19

EPISODE (1) Ms. 9¾-11

THE THREE STRETTO FUGUES
Contrapunctus V, Exposition Ms. 1-17

251

EPISODE (1) MS. 14-17

Exposition II, Ms. 17 to
33-1/4

252

EPISODE (2) MS. 30-33 1/4

Contrapunctus VI, Exposition I in Division One, Ms. 1-9

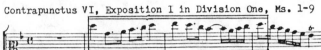

EPISODE (1) MS. 5½-7

EPISODE (1) Ms. 39½ - 42

EPISODE (2) Ms. 44-47

Contrapunctus VII, Exposition Ms. 1 to 13-1/2

258

Exposition II, Ms. 35-99

259

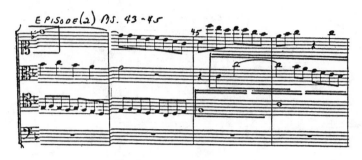

EPISODE (2) MS. 43-45

EPISODE (3) MS. 53-59   55

260

EPISODE (4) MS. 67-73

262

Contrapunctus X, Exposition I in Division One, Ms. (1)1/4 to 12

Exposition II in Division Two, Ms. 23-38

EPISODE (3) M.30

THE TWO TRIPLE FUGUES
Contrapunctus VIII, Exposition I in Division One, Ms. 1-17
EPISODE (1) Ms. 5-6½

Exposition II in Division Two,
Ms. 39-1/2 to 54

265

EPISODE (6-A) MS. 53-54

Exposition III in Division Three,
Ms. 94-1/4 to 117-1/4

EPISODE (10) MS. 98-99/4

EPISODE (11) MS. 103-105 1/4

EPISODE (12-A) MS. 109-117 1/4

Contrapunctus XI, Exposition I in Division One, Ms. 1-18

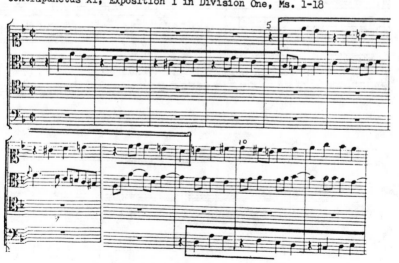

EPISODE (1-A) Ms. 17-18½

Exposition II in Division Two, Ms. 27-1/2 - 60

EPISODE (3) Ms. 31-34½

268

EPISODE (4) MS. 38-44

EPISODE (5) MS. 47-57

EPISODE (6-A)
MS. 60-61 1/4

Exposition IA in Division Three,
Ms. 71-1/4 to 89-1/2

EPISODE (7) MS. 75-76 1/4

270

EPISODE (8) Exposition III in Division Four,
MS. 88-89½ Ms. 89-1/2 to 109

EPISODE (9)
MS. 93¼-93¾

EPISODE (10) MS. 97-100

271

EPISODE (II)
109 MS. 109-111 3/4

THE TWO MIRROR FUGUES
Contrapunctus XVI, Ms. 1-13, rectus and inversus

Contrapunctus XVII, Ms. 1-21, rectus and inversus

EPISODE (I) ms. 9¼-10

EPISODE (2) MS. 18 – 21

THE QUADRUPLE FUGUE
Contrapunctus XVIII, Exposition I in Division One, Ms. 1 to 21-1/2

Exposition II in Division Two, Ms. 114-1/4 to 147-1/4

EPISODE (11) MS. 127¾-128¾

278

Exposition III in Division Three, B-A-C-H theme,
Ms. 193-1/2 to 207-1/4

EPISODE (17) MS. 197 1/4 - 201 1/2

THE COUNTER-SUBJECTS:

Tonal, real, free counter-subjects can vary with the fugue and fugue type. Motivically-fragmented counter-subjects leading to a possible "migrating" idea as seen in simple fugue Contrapunctus II need not be limited to a simple fugue type. The counter-subject procedures for the separate subjects in double, triple, and quadruple fugues can have complementary ideas. The counter-subject's motivic dependence on the subject can lead to significantly new procedures and expanded motives. New motives, whether tonal or chromatic, can give to the counter-subject a higher dimension of contrapuntal interest.

In fugues having more than one subject, as double, triple, and quadruple fugues, any one of the subjects can serve a counter-subject function to a second subject.

THE COUNTER-SUBJECTS

CONTRA-PUNCTUS	TYPE OF COUNTER-SUBJECT	BASES FOR MOTIVIC MATERIAL	DISTINCTIVE ATTRIBUTES
THE FOUR SIMPLE FUGUES			
I	Tonal CS in 2 voices, with reference to CS in third voice, in Expo. only	A new motive is introduced, which forms the basis of many episodes	
II	Essentially free, could be considered "migrating" CS	Primarily based on last measure of subject, in normal, inverted, and retrograde orders	(1)
III	Real, with chromatic elements	Outline of fugue subject found in CS, with chromatic passing notes; other motives based on motives from subject (2)	(3)
IV	Tonal	Repeated motive in first 2 Ms. based on the inversion of the last Ms. of the subject; other motives based on subject (4)	CS appears throughout most of the fugue, with frequent references by paired voices in imitation. (5) The CS is closely related contrapuntally to the episodes as in Ms. 61–63, or in paired imitation as in Ms. 65–67. Paired imitative free material is integrated frequently with paired stretto subject.
THE THREE STRETTO FUGUES			
V	Free		

282

THE COUNTER-SUBJECTS (continued)

CONTRA-PUNCTUS	TYPE OF COUNTER-SUBJECT	BASES FOR MOTIVIC MATERIAL	DISTINCTIVE ATTRIBUTES
(THE THREE STRETTO FUGUES)			
VI	Free		
VII	Free		
THE TWO DOUBLE FUGUES			
IX	Free for both subjects in their respective expositions		Subject II is never stated without Subject I, so that Subject I retains a certain function as a CS, although strict order in presentation of CS is not followed.
X	Free for both subjects		Occasionally motives from CS are stated within fugue, as the bass in Ms. 94–95, and alto in M. 129.
THE TWO TRIPLE FUGUES			
VIII	Each of the 3 subjects has its own procedures for a CS: Sub. I – real in Expo. only. Sub. II – serves as CS for Sub. I at the same time it is presented in its own Expo. II. Sub. III – Free	New material, with first motive presented in sequence, repeated in diminution and rhythmically altered, in relation to Sub. I.	After the succeeding two stretto statements as CS and Subject (6), the subjects are freely combined.

THE COUNTER-SUBJECTS (continued)

CONTRA-PUNCTUS	TYPE OF COUNTER-SUBJECT	BASES FOR MOTIVIC MATERIAL	DISTINCTIVE ATTRIBUTES
XI	Each of the 3 subjects has its own procedures for a CS: Sub. I – Free Sub. II – new "chromatic motive", stated most frequently with Sub. II	New "chromatic motive"	This new "chromatic motive" follows neither strict rules for a CS nor a new subject presented within an exposition. The function appears to be for chromatic (?) harmonic and contrapuntal coloring.
	Sub. III – Free, but Sub. III frequently stated in stretto with Subs. I or II		

THE TWO MIRROR FUGUES

XVI	Free		
XVII	Free, with an approach to a CS in Expo. only		

THE QUADRUPLE FUGUE

XVIII	Free, for all three subjects		

FOOTNOTES FOR CHART OF COUNTER-SUBJECT

(1) The counter-subject is theoretically free throughout this fugue. However, an unusual usage of the motives taken from the first counter-subject presented by the bass in Ms. 5 to 9-1/2 is found. This first counter-subject is frequently heard with later entrances of the subject and answer, but in "migrating" procedure, i.e., motives from the original counter-subject proceed from voice to voice, rather than remaining in one voice. While this migrating procedure is not consistent throughout this fugue, it occurs in a sufficient number of examples to warrant further study.

The original order of the counter-subject as stated by the bass is shown in the following example. Ms. 31 to 35-1/2 illustrate how this same counter-subject can be seen to migrate from voice to voice.

M.5

Bass

M.31

The following is a listing of the counter-subject as it appears as a migrating counter-subject, based entirely or partially on the first presentation by the bass:

ORDER OF ENTRIES OF MIGRATING COUNTER-SUBJECTS

FUGUE STATEMENT	VOICE PART	MEASURE NUMBERS	COUNTER-SUBJECT	MEASURE NUMBERS
Subject	B	1-5	Bass (complete)	5-9
Answer	T	5-9	Fragmented figures only	
Subject	A	9-13	Fragmented figures only	
Answer	S	13-17	Fragmented figures only	
Subject	A	23-27	B, T	25-28
Answer	S	26-30	T	27-28 (same as above)
Subject	B	31-35	S, T, A, S	31-35
Answer	T	38-42	A, B, A, S	38-42
Subject	S	45-49	(T, A,) A, T	(45) 46-49
Subject	A	49-53	B	51-52
Subject	B	(52) 53-57	A, S (last motive delayed)	53-1/2 to 56
Subject	B	61-65	S, A, S	61-64
Answer	T	69-73	A, S, A	71-73
Subject	S	79-83	B, T, B, T, B	79-82

The above listing includes all statements of the subject and answer in this fugue.

(2)

286

(3) A listing of the order of entries of the counter-subject follows:

SECTION	MEASURE NO.	FUGUE STATEMENT	VOICE	KEY	COUNTER-SUBJECT
I	1	Subject	T	d	
	5	Answer	A	d	T
	9	Subject	S	d	A
	15	Answer	B	d	S
A	23-1/4	Answer	S	d	A
	29-1/4	Answer	T	a	A
	35-1/4	Answer	T	F	A (modified)
II	43	Answer	S	a	A
	51	Answer	B	g	S
B	55	Answer	A	d	T
	58	Subject	S	d	T (abbreviated)
III	63	Answer	T	d	B

All statements of the counter-subject in the main fugue sections I, II, and III follow the conventional order, with the exception of the soprano answer in M. 43, which has accompanying it the counter-subject stated in the alto, rather than the bass (from M. 15). This usage of the alto voice may have been prompted by the three statements of the counter-subject in Intermediate Section A directly preceding the soprano answer in M. 43.

(4)

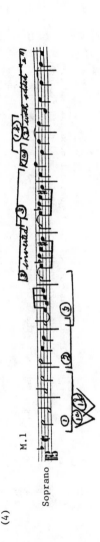

M.1

Soprano

(5) The counter-subject appears throughout most of the fugue, but numerous modified entrances occur, as well as paired imitative references. The counter-subject is frequently presented in paired imitation between two voices, as in Ms. 65-67. No counter-subject exists for two entrances of the fugue subject: the alto subject in Ms. 31-35, and the tenor subject in Ms. 129-133.

The counter-subject is frequently anticipated by an episode preceding it, as in Ms. 63-64. The imitative motives between the soprano and alto lead directly without interruption to the presentation of the counter-subject in paired imitation between the soprano and alto in Ms. 65-67.

In Ms. 107-109 the imitative counter-subject alternating between soprano and alto serves as a fitting complement to the tight stretto statement of the subject. Paired imitative free material is carefully integrated with the paired stretto subject. Ms. 111-115 have similar paired procedures as Ms. 107-109.

ORDER OF ENTRIES OF THE COUNTER-SUBJECT OF CONTRAPUNCTUS IV

FUGUE STATEMENT	VOICE	MEASURE NUMBERS	COUNTER-SUBJECT	MEASURE NUMBERS
Subject	S	1-5		
Answer	A	5-9	S	5-9
Subject	T	11-15	A	12-14
Answer	B	15-19	T, same as Soprano above	15-19
				28 only
Subject	S	27-31	A	
Subject	A	31-35	NO CS	
Subject	T	35-39	A	35-38
Subject	B	39-43	T, modified	39-41
Subject	B	61-65	A, imitating S	61-63
Subject	T	65-69	A, imitating S	65-67
Subject	A	73-77	T, reference only	72-74

288

ORDER OF ENTRIES OF THE CS OF CONTRAPUNCTUS IV (continued)

FUGUE STATEMENT	VOICE	MEASURE NUMBERS	COUNTER-SUBJECT	MEASURE NUMBERS
Subject	S	77-81	A, reference only, similar to T CS, Ms. 72-73	77-78
Subject	T & B	107-111	Imitative reference between S and A	107-109
Answer	S & A	111-115	Imitative reference between T and B	111-113
Subject	T	129-133	NO CS	
Subject	A	133-137	Brief imitative reference between S and T	133-134

(6) The order of entries is as follows:

Exposition II	Ms. 39-1/2 to 43(1/2)	Subject I	Soprano	
	Ms. 39-1/4 to 42	Subject II	Alto	(CS)
	Ms. 43-1/2 to 47(1/2)	Subject I	Bass	
	Ms. 43-3/4 to 46	Answer II	Soprano	(CS)
	Ms. 49-1/2 to 53(1/2)	Answer I	Alto	
	Ms. 49-3/4 to 52	Subject II	Bass	(CS)

Subject II continues to serve as a counter-subject for the proper voice of Subject I or Answer I for the next two stretto statements in Sections IVA and IVB, but thereafter, the subjects are freely combined. While the exact procedure for a counter-subject is not followed throughout this fugue, sufficient attention to Subject II serving as a counter-subject for Subject I is given that at least mention should be made of this dual nature of Subject II.

(7) The chromatic passage which is heard both ascending and descending with the first statement of Subject II appears to be a counter-subject, but its procedure does not follow strict rules for treatment of a counter-subject. Its function seems to be for chromatic coloring, both harmonically and contrapuntally. Nor can this chromatic motive be considered a subject for a separate fughetta because of the same lack of adherence to contrapuntal rules.

The chromatic passage is partially heard in Division One following the first statement of the answer by the soprano in Ms. 9-10, and stated in its entirety toward the end of Division One in the alto, in Ms. 25-1/4 to 26-1/2. This last descending statement is the inverted form of the chromatic motive. This descending chromatic passage in the alto precedes the first statement of Subject II by the alto in Exposition II. The soprano statement of the chromatic passage in Ms. 28-1/2 to 30 could be imitation by inversion of the same chromatic passage in Ms. 25-1/4 to 26-1/2, so that the chromatic passage is fully prepared. In these two cases, the function of this chromatic passage seems to be harmonic and contrapuntal coloring.

This chromatic passage will be called a "Chromatic Motive" in this study, bearing in mind that it is stated most frequently with Subject II. The Chromatic Motive is stated in many ways, both extended and abbreviated. The result of using this Chromatic Motive heightens the chromatic harmonic background. To emphasize chromatic harmony was the intent in Contrapunctus III, but the harmony remained chromatic throughout the fugue. This Contrapunctus XI is the first fugue in Die Kunst der Fuge to have the chromatic harmony brought about by means of a chromatic motive.

The chromatic motive adds to the contrapuntal interest, since this chromatic motive changes the coloring of the subject with which it is combined.

A full listing of the entries of the Chromatic Motive as used in Division Two follows. The listing includes only those statements that are patterned after the first three statements: in the soprano, Ms. 28-1/2 to 30, ascending from tonic to dominant, 8 notes; in the bass, Ms. 30-1/4 to 32, descending from dominant to tonic, 7 notes; and in the alto, Ms. 32-1/2 to 33-3/4, descending from tonic to dominant, 6 notes.

Chr. M.   -   Chromatic Motive
normal   -   ascending

290

DIVISION TWO

MEASURE NOS.	FUGUE STATEMENT	VOICE	ORDER	STARTING NOTE	KEY
27-1/2 to 31	Subject II	A	inverted	dominant	d
28-1/2 to 30	Chr. M.	S	normal	tonic	d
30-1/4 to 32	Chr. M.	B	inverted	dominant	d
32-1/2 to 33-3/4	Chr. M.	A	inverted	tonic	d
34-1/2 to 38	Answer II	T	inverted	dominant	a
35-1/4 to 37	Chr. M.	B	normal	tonic	a
37-1/4 to 39	Chr. M.	S	inverted	dominant	a
	(rhythmically altered)				
43-3/4 to 47	Subject II	B	inverted	dominant	d
44-1/4 to 47-1/2	Chr. M.	T	normal	tonic	d
	(extended to full chromatic scale, with all 12 notes)				
54-1/4 to 56	Chr. M.	S	inverted	dominant	d
55-1/4 to 56-1/2	Chr. M.	B	inverted	tonic	d
	(with added notes preceding and following the basic motive)				
57-60	Answer II	S	normal	tonic	d
57-1/4 to 59	Chr. M.	T	inverted	dominant	d
59(1/4) to 61	Chr. M.	B	inverted	dominant	d modulates
	End of Exposition II				
65-1/4 to 67-1/4	Chr. M.	T	inverted	dominant	a
	(rhythmically altered)				
67-3/4 to 71	Answer II	B	normal	dominant	a
68-1/4 to 70	Chr. M.	S	inverted	dominant	a
	End of Division Two				

It can be seen from the above listing that the Chromatic Motive is combined freely with Subject II and Answer II. The Chromatic Motive is stated by itself in this division, and in stretto with itself. Numerous smaller chromatic figures occur which add to the chromatic harmony.

Numerous stretto passages occur later in the fugue that combine some form of the Chromatic Motive with the main subjects of this fugue. In Ms. 115 to 117-1/2, the bass has the normal order of the Chromatic Motive extended to ten notes of the chromatic scale, below Subject II inverted and Subject III in retrograde. The tenor follows immediately in Ms. 117-1/2 to 120-3/4 with an inverted extension of the Chromatic Motive for ten notes of the chromatic scale, rhythmically altered, with two stretto statements of Subject III in normal order.

Numerous such stretto usages of the Chromatic Motive can be found, but large sections exist in this fugue with little or no reference to this Chromatic Motive. The symmetrical procedure as exists for the other subjects and counter-subjects in this study is what is omitted in the use of the Chromatic Motive. It seems best to consider its harmonic and contrapuntal coloring as its chief function.

The Chromatic Motive is stated in the bass in the coda, as a transition proceeding from the end of Section XIIA, throughout Episode (20), and to the start of Section XIIB. In this passage the Chromatic Motive is rhythmically altered. A last touch of chromatic coloring is stated in Section XIIB by the inclusion of an extended Chromatic Motive in diminution in eighth-notes, together with the triple stretto statement of the three subjects in M. 181.

FOOTNOTES FOR CHAPTER THREE

(1) Gräser, Wolfgang, "Bachs 'Kunst der Fuge'", in Bach Jahrbuch (1924), pp. 1 ff.

CHAPTER FOUR
THE EPISODES, FREE MATERIAL, AND CODAS

THE EPISODES:

The function of the episodes, together with the free material, can include lightening of texture; providing transitional passages; independent styles and textures; climactic cadences; the development of symmetrical schemes in the overall planning of the episodes; and numerous other procedures. The term "free material" as used in this chapter is meant to refer to parts progressing in a free contrapuntal style. This term is distinguished from "new material", meaning new motivic material not specifically based on a significant motive.

THE FOUR SIMPLE FUGUES: Each of the four simple fugues has distinctly different procedures for its episodes and free material, varying from a close motivic relationship to the subject to a complete independence of structure. Since the simple fugues have but one subject and a limited usage of stretto statements, the episodes can assume weighty dimensions.

C. No.	EPISODE NO. AND MEASURES	GENERAL DESCRIPTION
I		OVERALL STRUCTURE: The episodes are primarily imitative, based on CS(1) and motives of the Sub. The reduction to 3 voices in all episodes but the last gives to the episode a transitional function. The silent voice in each of the 3-voice episodes is the voice in which the Sub. next appears, with the exception of the B Ans. in M. 32. In most cases, beginning with the final Ans. in the Expo., the voice which completes the statement of the Sub. or Ans. continues as one of the two imitative voices in the episode. The length of the 6 episodes varies, with the last episode being the longest.
	(1) Ms. 17–23 3 voices	Tonal canonic imitation between T and S at the distance of a 7th after 2 beats, starting with the T in Ms. 17. The T continues with the inverted CS(1), while the S draws upon figures from motives from the Sub. The B proceeds by sequence based on

C. No.	EPISODE NO. AND MEASURES	GENERAL DESCRIPTION
(I)	(1)	various versions of CS(1). The A is silent.
	(2) Ms. 27-29 3 voices	Real canonic imitation exists between T and A at the distance of a 5th after 2 beats, starting with the T in M. 26-1/2. The B is partially sequential, based on CS(1). S is silent.
	(3) Ms. 36-40 3 voices	Tonal canonic imitation between A and B at the distance of a 7th after 2 beats, based on CS(1). This canon is similar to the canon in Episode (1). The S uses inversions of CS(1) in chain construction. T is silent.
	(4) Ms. 44-49 3 voices	The A, T, and B draw upon CS(1) in tight stretto combinations, with the T ending with motives from the Sub. These 3 voices are basically imitative, although a few Ms. of canon between A and T in Ms. 44-46 exist at the distance of a 6th after 1 beat. S is silent.
	(5) Ms. 53-56 3 voices	3 voices basically imitative drawing upon motives from the Sub. B is silent.
	(6) Ms. 60-74 4 voices	This last episode before the coda has a climactic function by being the only episode with 4 voices, and being the longest. Imitation exists in inversion between B and T in Ms. 60-63, based on Sub. (3). A pedal point begins in M. 63 in the B, and after a brief silence in the T, all three upper voices combine in constant imitation based on CS(1). Following a deceptive cadence in M. 66, which ends the B pedal point, B and T continue in tonal canonic imitation to M. 70, at the ultimate distance of a 6th after 2 beats. The usage of CS(1) is again similar to Episode (1). This Episode (6) ends with a climactic chord which might call for a cadenza improvised.
II		OVERALL STRUCTURE: The majority of the 8 episodes are imitative in varying orders

C. No.	EPISODE NO. AND MEASURES	GENERAL DESCRIPTION
(II)		and combinations, based on Sub.(3), with occasional usage of other motives from the Sub. and CS. Pedal point, soprano melodic interest, and a thinning imitative texture with rests, are all used for symmetrical development of the episodes.
	(1) Ms. 17-23 4 voices	
	(1-A) 17-21	S has 2 successive pedal points. A and T proceed by sequence in pairs, and B is sequential.
	(1-B) 21-23	S has increased melodic interest, the B begins with pedal point, and then all 3 lower voices support the S with a chordal background. Episode (1-B) ends the Expo.
	(2) M. 30 3 voices	This 1 Ms. imitative episode separates the stretto statement in Sec. II from the next statement of the Sub.
	(3) Ms. 35-37 4 voices, with rests	Consistent imitative entrances between the 4 voices occur, in circular fashion, beginning and ending with the S: S - T - A - B - T - S. Each new voice in imitation begins after 2 beats.
	(4) Ms. 42-45 3 voices	All voices are basically imitative, based on Ans.(3) in M. 41.
	(5) Ms. 57-60 4 voices, with some rests	An increased imitative movement occurs, based on CS(1). A figure from this motive is heard in mirror imitation in M. 59.
	(6) Ms. 65-69 3 voices	A thinning imitative texture takes place, with the T remaining silent for the last 3 Ms. before its next statement of the Ans.
	(7) Ms. 73-79 4 voices	
	(7-A) 73-76	A and T are imitative; B and S are partially imitative.
	(7-B) 76-79	Similar to Episode (1-B), the S has the concentration of melodic interest, while the B has a pedal point, and the 2 inner parts supply the chordal background.

C. No.	EPISODE NO. AND MEASURES	GENERAL DESCRIPTION
(II)	(7)	Episode (7) has been planned to relate to Episode (1) because this Episode (7) concludes the fugue proper before the entrance of the coda in M. 79.
	(8) Ms. 83–84 4 voices	A similarity can be found to exist between this episode and Episode (1-A). The S has a pedal point, the A and B have a brief imitative motive, and the A and T finally proceed in parallel 3rds to complete the cadence.
III		OVERALL STRUCTURE: Episode (1) sets the basic pattern for the 8 episodes of imitation based on Sub.(3). Episodes (2) and (5) have a trio sonata texture. The remaining episodes are transitional.
	(1) Ms. 13–15 3 voices	Imitation exists between all voices based on Sub.(3), leading directly to the last statement of the Ans. by B. The B is silent.
	(2) Ms. 19-1/4 to 23-1/4 3 voices	Episodes (2) and (5) have the texture of a trio sonata, with imitation in the upper two voices and continuous bass movement. In Episode (2) the S and A proceed in strict canonic imitation at the distance of a 4th after 1 Ms., beginning with the A in M. 19 based on motives from the CS. The B proceeds in sequence with a chromatic motive taken from the CS. The texture of this episode is carried over into the Intermediate Section (A), which retains a 3-voice texture. The T is silent.
	(3) Ms. 27 to 29-1/4 3 voices	The same trio texture is continued, retaining imitation between the upper voices and sequence in the B. The T is silent until its entrance.
	(4) Ms. 33 to 35-1/4 3 voices	All voices are individually sequential. Mirror imitation is created successively between A and B, and T and B. S is silent.
	(5) Ms. 39-1/4 to 43 3 voices	Having the texture of a trio sonata, a short phrase between T and A exists in canonic imitation at the 6th after 4 beats,

C.	EPISODE NO.	
No.	AND MEASURES	GENERAL DESCRIPTION

(III) (5)　　　　　　　　　based on CS(1), beginning with the T in
M. 39-1/4. This same phrase is imitated
again starting a major 2nd higher beginning
with the T in M. 41-1/4. The B is
sequential, and S remains silent.

(6) Ms. 47-51　　　This is a tightly-knit episode with all
3 voices　　　voices in continuous movement. Although
the combinations change, 2 voices proceed
in parallel movement, with the third voice
in mirror imitation. The B is silent.

(7) M. 62　　　　The 3 voices are partly imitative in normal
3 voices　　　and mirror orders. T is silent.

(8) Ms. 67-72
4 voices
　(8-A) 67-70　　In short imitative passages, Sec. III is
brought to a close, leading to the coda.
The B has a pedal point.
　(8-B) 70-72　　The brief coda continues the short imitative passages of Episode (8-A), with a
gradual reduction in rhythmic and melodic
interest. The T and A extend the cadence
in M. 72, which two voices began this
fugue. The subdominant is emphasized.

IV　　　　　　　　　　　OVERALL STRUCTURE: The episodes in this
fugue are developed to such an extent that
their weight is equal to that of the Sub.,
Ans., and CS. Many sections of the lengthy
episodes are not only based on paired
imitation, but the imitation results from
each voice progressing individually by
sequence. Frequently a free voice is
paired in imitation with the CS, or at the
end of the CS, the free voice continues in
paired imitation in the episode. The two
stretto statements of the Sub. and Ans. in
Sec. IV include no episodes, thus giving
climactic preference to the Sub. rather
than the 7 episodes. A descending 3rd
motive from Sub.(1b) is frequently heard.

(1) Ms. 9-1/4　　Individual sequence in S and A continues
to 11　　　the last motives of the Sub. and CS.
2 voices

C.	EPISODE NO.	
No.	AND MEASURES	GENERAL DESCRIPTION

(IV)   (2) Ms. 19-27

      (2-A) 19-23
      4 voices
All voices individually sequential, resulting in imitation in pairs; S and A based on descending 3rds; T and B imitate short motives by inversion.

      (2-B) 23-27
      3 voices
All voices individually sequential, with T and A proceeding by imitation in inversion, and B following a sequential motive outlining a triad.

      (3) Ms. (42)
      43-61
      4 voices
All voices are individually sequential throughout the four subdivisions of Episode (3).

      (3-A) 42-47
The paired voices in imitation are the reverse of Episode (2-A), with T and B based on descending thirds, and S and A proceeding by imitation in inversion.

      (3-B) 47-53
All sequential motives are taken from the Sub.

      (3-C) 53-57
Imitation in pairs results, with S and B having descending 3rds, and A and T imitating short motives in normal order. These same motives are again found in Episode (5-B) with contrasting paired voices.

      (3-D) 57-61
      4 voices
      reduced to
      3 voices
The motive of a descending 3rd is first stated in the B starting with M. 56-3/4, and then imitated by all four voices in this order: B, T, A, and S. This process of imitation serves as a dissolution of the paired voices in imitation in cadential manner leading to the next entrance of the Sub. in the B in M. 61.

      (4) Ms. 69-73
      3 voices
Voices individually sequential, with T and A imitative using the inversion of the descending 3rd, or ascending 6th, followed by one descending 3rd in imitation. The B has its own sequential motives in continuous movement.

      (5) Ms. 81-107
      (5-A) 81-87
      4 voices
The first subdivision of Episode (5) concludes Sec. III of this fugue. The S, in sequence, proceeds to its pedal point leading to a cadence in C Major in M. 87. The B and A proceed primarily in mirror imitation. The T is free, but partially

C. No.	EPISODE NO. AND MEASURES	GENERAL DESCRIPTION
(IV)	(5)	imitative with the other 3 voices.
	(5-B) 87 to 90-1/2 4 voices	The interval of a descending 3rd is imitated in succession by S and T, S and A, and S and T. The remaining 2 voices have short imitative passages.
	(5-C) 90-1/2 to 97-1/2 4 voices	From here to the end of Episode (5), each of the voices is basically sequential. In (5-C) the inclusion of numerous rests in the measures creates a transparent texture. By way of contrast of (5-B), Episode (5-C) has constant changes in the combinations of imitative voices, and the order of the motive changes, such as normal and inverted orders.
	(5-D) 97-1/2 to 103 4 voices, with rests	S has its own sequential motive, and the A and T are somewhat imitative. The motive for the sequential B outlines a series of triads, which in turn includes imitative intervals of descending 3rds.
	(5-E) 103-107 4 voices, with rests	This subdivision starts with imitation in pairs, the B and S having descending 3rds, and the A and T short motives. Soon the voices are interchanged, and a gradual dissolution of the imitative pairs leads to the climactic stretto statements of the Sub. and Ans.
		Episodes (3) and (5) are the longest of the episodes and retain a similar structure. The mirror imitation in Episode (5), as well as varying voices in pairs, preserves a distinction between these two episodes.
	(6) Ms. 115-129 4 voices	Frequent rests create a lighter texture to this entire episode. All voices are basically individually sequential.
	(6-A) 115- 119	All voices imitate at some point the motive of the descending 3rd, and the upper voices imitate the preceding motive of the B in M. 114 in constantly changing voices.
	(6-B) 119 to 124-1/2	Other than the descending 3rd stated by the A in sequence, the other voices have new short motives stated in sequence. The new motives are based on different orders of motives from the S (or CS). The interval of a 4th in the S is the inverted first figure of the Sub. The B combines a small figure from Sub.(3) with the

C. No.	EPISODE NO. AND MEASURES	GENERAL DESCRIPTION

(IV)   (6)
(cont.) retrograde order of the complete Sub.(3). The S and A could be said to be paired, as well as the T and B.

(6-C), Ms. 124-1/2 to 129
The S and A are similar to the T and B in Episode (6-B), while the T and B are similar to the S and A. The A is the inversion of the B in (6-B). A dissolution of the imitative and sequential procedures, as well as a reduction in the number of voices to two in M. 128, leads to the Coda in M. 129.

(7), Ms. 137-138, 4 voices
This brief episode concludes the fugue by extension and sequence, based on the motives in M. 136.

THE THREE STRETTO FUGUES: Despite the increasingly dense stretto statements in the three stretto fugues, the weight and complexity of the episodes and free material vary with each stretto fugue, and ingeniously contribute to the structure of each fugue.

C. No.	EPISODE NO. AND MEASURES	GENERAL DESCRIPTION

V
OVERALL STRUCTURE: The eight episodes are primarily found at ends of sections, and occasionally included after two voices as a subdivision of one section. The fifth and sixth episodes have two distinctly imitative passages, which will be called "intermediate episodes". A close motivic relationship exists between the Sub. and the material for the episodes and free material. The episodes in each of the first five major sections of this fugue are given an individual contrapuntal treatment, thereby contributing to the gradation of climax between the sections.

(1) Ms. 14-17 4 voices
Free material is included based on imitation of motives from the Sub. to conclude the Expo. A pedal point in the B exists as part of the final cadence. The figure for the last two beats of M. 16 in the B serves as an anacrusis to Section II.

300

C.	EPISODE NO.	
No.	AND MEASURES	GENERAL DESCRIPTION

(V)   (2) Ms. 30 to 33-1/4 3 voices — Each voice proceeds in individual sequence, resulting in imitation between all three voices. The S is silent.

(3) Ms. 37-1/2 to 41 — Four voices begin in Ms. 37-1/2 to 38-1/2. The upper three voices are imitative above the B in sequence. Three voices continue from M. 38-3/4, with the upper 2 voices proceeding with chords in suspension, the S resolving to a consonant interval on the weak beat of each measure. The B has continuous movement which is partially sequential. The T is silent.

(4) Ms. 45-1/2 to 47 4 voices — This episode serves as a transition for the modulation to B-flat Major in Sec. IVA.

(5) Ms. 52-1/2 to 57 4 voices — Ms. 52-1/2 to 53-1/4 conclude Sec. IVA. The first intermediate episode occurs from M. 53-1/4 to the B in M. 58. The intermediate episode is a double canon between the S and T, followed by the A and B, each voice entering after 1 beat. The 4 voices have but one alteration in the main canonic theme, the "b-flat" in the A and B in M. 55. Because of the similarities of the 4 voices, this imitative passage could be called a quadruple canon at the octave and 4th below the Sub., with each entrance after 1 beat. This intermediate episode serves as a practical application of canonic principles in the structure of the fugue, as well as affords contrapuntal contrast.

(6) Ms. 62-1/2 to 69 4 voices

  (6-A) 62-1/2 to 65 — By imitation in the upper 3 voices, and an ascending chromatic passage in the B, Sec. IV is brought to a close.

  (6-B) 65-69 4 voices — This second intermediate episode is similar in structure to Episode (5), but the basic Sub. of the canon is inverted. This new quadruple canon could be described as follows:

S followed by B after 1 beat, a 12th
  below, worked at the 5th;
B followed by A after 1 beat, an
  octave above the B;
A followed by T after 1 beat, a
  fifth below the A;

Following the canonic intermediate section,
the voices conclude with figures in sequence and imitation taken from the canon,
and lead directly to Sec. V.

(7) Ms. 74-77   The B is sequential, with the T partially
    3 voices   in imitation to the B. The S is free, and
the A is silent. This episode comes be-
tween two stretto statements of first the
Sub. and then the Ans. in Sec. V. A
climactic function is achieved with larger
intervallic skips in its motives.

(8) Ms. 82-86   This final episode serves to conclude Sec.
    4 voices   V; ends the episode material of this fugue;
and ushers in the coda. These functions are
accomplished by larger intervallic skips
within the motives, by irregular turns
within the motives, by heightened chromaticism, by increased movement within the
4 voices, and by syncopated rhythm in the
B in M. 85.

VI   OVERALL STRUCTURE: The episodes are
primarily used between major sections as
transitions, but in the 2 expositions,
episodes do occur after the first 3 voices
and before the entrance of the 4th voice.
The longest episodes exist between the 2nd
and 3rd sections in Division Two, and before
the coda. Although the Sub. has an added
dotted rhythm in normal note values, the
episodes and free material are the areas
where the greatest inclusion of rhythmic
variety occurs. Frequently two or three
voices imitate each other with rhythmic
figurations, while a 3rd or 4th voice
states the Sub. or Ans, as in Ms. 18-24.
Here the free material seems to serve as
an accompaniment to the Sub. Occasionally

302

C. No.	EPISODE NO. AND MEASURES	GENERAL DESCRIPTION

(VI)

(cont.) the free material anticipates the rhythmical figurations of an episode, as in Ms. 50-51, or Ms. 59-63. Numerous instances arise where a free voice has a false entry of a Sub., as in the A in M. 47.

Despite the distinct rhythmic interest reserved for the episodes and free material, the statements of the Sub. and Ans. seem more weighty because of the complex double and triple stretto sections. The episodes and free material govern the French style of the fugue. The motives for the episodes and free material are based on motives of the Sub. The addition of rhythmic figurations seem to embellish these motives, and add rhythmic contrast to the Sub. Strict and free imitation govern the procedures of the motives.

DIVISION ONE,
Ms. 1-34

(1) Ms. 5-1/2
to 7
3 voices

S and A are imitative and proceed in pairs. The B is sequential. The T is silent.

(2) Ms. 12-1/2
to 15
3 voices

The three upper voices are imitative with rhythmic figurations. The B is silent.

(3) M. 20-1/4
1 beat
2 voices

This 1 beat episode serves as a brief transition from Sec. III to Sec. IV. A quarter-note rest occurs in the T voice to separate the 2 consecutive statements by the T from M. 16 to 24-1/2.

(4) M. 24-3/4
1 beat
2 voices

This 1 beat separates the single statement of the Ans. with normal note values from the next 2 stretto statements in Sec. IV.

(5) Ms. 29-31
3 voices

The 3 voices are individually sequential, the S and A resulting in imitation. The T is silent.

303

C. No.	EPISODE NO. AND MEASURES	GENERAL DESCRIPTION
(VI)	DIVISION TWO Ms. 35-79	
	(1) Ms. 39-1/2 to 42 3 then 2 voices	The T and S begin in imitation, and then the S is imitated by the B. The B is sequential. A and T are omitted in the 2-part structure.
	(2) Ms. 44-47 3 voices	Upper 2 voices are partially imitative, with the B being primarily sequential. The T is silent.
	(3) Ms. (50) 51-57 4 voices, with rests, then 3 voices	This episode is one of the two longest episodes in this fugue. Starting with M. 50-1/2 in the upper 2 voices, the episode is basically 4 voices to M. 54-1/2, although numerous rests occur. The B is sequential, while the upper 3 voices are imitative based on short-rhythmic motives. The upper 3 voices are also individually sequential.
	(4) Ms. 62 to 63-1/2 2 voices	The A creates a 2-voice canon with the B after 1 beat, at the distance of one octave. The canonic Sub. is sequential, having consecutive 16th notes, not rhythmic figurations.
	(5) Ms. 68-1/2 to 74-1/2 4 voices	Each voice is individually sequential, resulting in some imitation between the voices. While a complex rhythmic structure exists, the 4 voices combine in the same dotted rhythm as the last motive of the Sub. with normal note values, for almost 2 measures, leading to climactic chords, the last of which is extended with a fermata. Following the fermata, an elaborate anacrusis exists, leading to the same dotted rhythm in all 4 voices. The episode ends in M. 74-1/2 on the chord beginning the coda.
VII		OVERALL STRUCTURE: The four short episodes in this fugue serve to divide the intricate stretto statements into two main units, and serve to separate the smaller sections and add a coda.

C. No.	EPISODE NO. AND MEASURES	GENERAL DESCRIPTION
(VII)	(1) Ms. 19-20 4 voices	This episode serves as a brief transition between Secs. II and III. Short motives are imitated in normal and inverted orders.
	(2) Ms. 31-1/2 to 35	The fugue is divided into two units by this episode. The last motive of the Sub. in M. 31 is imitated by changing voices. A chromatic passing note is heard between motives as in M. 32 in the T, 3rd and 4th beats. A brief sequence occurs in the S in Ms. 32-33. The episode is reduced to 3 voices, the A being omitted. The episode is further lightened by having the B state eighth notes with eighth-note rests as a discontinuous line, in M. 33.
	(3) M. 49-3/4 1 beat 3 voices	This brief imitative episode is a 1 beat transition between Secs. V and VI.
	(4) Ms. 58-61 4 voices with coda	
	(4-A) 58-60	Completing the fugue before the coda, Episode (4-A) has numerous climactic techniques: punctuated chords are written beneath a melodic S line; 5 voices are heard, continuing the 5-voice texture begun in M. 56; and the underlying harmonies become increasingly more chromatic.
	(4-B) CODA Ms. 60-61 4 voices	Following an intensely-complex fugal structure with short episodes, and following a highly chromatic harmonic texture in Episode (4-A), this brief coda serves to resolve the tension. Chromatic half-steps occur between motives; imitation between voices takes place; and the B has a pedal point for 1-1/2 measures.

Because this fugue retains a basic 4-part texture, the free material is important. From M. 5 to the end of Sec. I, the free voices proceed by imitation of short motives in normal and inverted orders. These voices in paired imitation afford contrapuntal contrast to the stretto statements of the Sub. and Ans. The free

C.	EPISODE NO.	
No.	AND MEASURES	GENERAL DESCRIPTION

(VII) (4)

(cont.) material in the B in Ms. 25-26 creates a rhythmic sequence to add to the movement lacking in the augmented Sub. stated by the T. At the end of Sec. III at the mid-point of the fugue, large inter-vallic leaps in the S in M. 30 add tension to the climax. The B has a continuous 16th note passage to support the three-voice stretto statement in Ms. 38-41, and to support the two-voice stretto in Ms. 45-47. The free material thus offers contrapuntal contrast to the tight stretto statements of the Sub. and Ans. in various ways.

Only 10 measures exist in the entire fugue in 3-part texture:

> 2-1/4 measures in Sec. II;
> 3 measures in Episode (2);
> 5 measures in Sec. V; and a few parts of individual measures throughout the fugue.

From M. 5 with the entrance of the 4th voice in the Expo., a 4-part texture con-tinues throughout Sec. I. While rests do occur within this lengthy section, not a sufficient number to justify describing this texture as anything but 4-part. The same is true of Secs. III, IV, and VI. The omitted voice in Episode (2) prepares for the entrance of the A Ans. in augmen-tation in M. 35, as does the omitted voice prepare for the entrance of the S Sub. in augmentation in M. 50, after Episode (3). Toward the end of Sec. VI and continuing through the 1st part of Episode (4), the texture becomes more transparent. The episode changes texture with concentration on the melodic line and chordal accompani-ment. This change in texture draws attention to the coda in the last part of Episode (4).

THE DOUBLE AND TRIPLE FUGUES: The presentation of the two subjects in double counterpoint and the

three subjects in triple counterpoint is the chief interest in the double and triple fugues. Since no distinct fughettas exist for the presentation of the two
subjects in either double fugue, the episodes follow
basically the same procedures throughout the two fugues.
The triple fugues show greater attention to the episodes
for the individual fughettas for the respective three
subjects.

C. No.	EPISODE NO. AND MEASURES	GENERAL DESCRIPTION

THE TWO DOUBLE FUGUES

IX

OVERALL STRUCTURE: Because of the length
of the 2 subjects, the episodes and free
material have a subservient function. No
episode exists in Expo. I. A transitory
episode is included at the end of Expo. I
and between each stretto statement of the
2 subjects. Motives from Sub. I and the
last measure of Sub. II are the bases for
the motives in the episodes and free
material. Various imitative devices are
used, as well as sequence in individual
voices.

(1) Ms. 29-35
3 voices

Sub. (4) of Sub. I is the basis for this
imitative episode. Following the completion of the T Ans. I at the end of the
Expo., Sub.(4) is imitated by the S, then
B, and A. The T then proceeds in sequence. The additional added parts are
free. First the A is silent to M. 31-3/4,
then the T is silent. Episode (1) ends on
a deceptive cadence in D Minor, leading
directly to the entrance of Sub. II in M.
35.

(2) Ms. 44-45
3 voices

ISub. (4) is imitated first by the A, then
the T. IISub.(3) is then imitated by the
A. Since S and T have just completed their
Subs. II and I respectively, the A is
given the imitative motives of both subjects. The B is silent.

(3) Ms. 53-59
3 voices

A similarity can be seen between Fig.(4-B)
of Sub. I and IISub.(3). The eighth notes
used in Fig.(4-B) of Sub. I could be considered IISub.(3) in diminution. Since
the S and A continue in 8th-note movement,

307

C.	EPISODE NO.	
No.	AND MEASURES	GENERAL DESCRIPTION

(IX)   (3)   (cont.) it might be best to consider these 2 voices as being based on Fig.(4-B) of Sub. I, imitated in inversion and sequence. The T continues in sequence based on Sub.II. The entire ISub.(4) is then stated by the S and imitated by the T. The A continues the sequence of IISub.(3) in inversion. Ms. 55-56 could be considered as augmented statement of Sub. II, Motive (3), in the T. The B continues to be silent.

(4) Ms. 67-73   ISub.(4) is heard in imitation and sequence
    3 voices,   by the S and A. The B continues in se-
    with rests   quence based on the inversion of IISub.(3). The T is silent. With the numerous rests, the number of voices is reduced to two for 3 beats in Ms. 70 and 72.

(5) Ms. 81-89,   ISub.(3) is used as the first sequential
    3 voices,   motive in the T. The T then continues with
    with some   a new motive in sequence. The A and S
    rests   proceed by imitation and sequence, with the S having a false entry of Sub. II in Ms. 85-87. The T joins the S in M. 88 in pairs in parallel 6ths based on ISub.(4). The B is silent.

(6) Ms. 97-99   ISub.(4) is heard in the S, imitated by T
    3 voices   and B in parallel 6ths. The A is silent.

(7) Ms. 107-   This is the longest of the episodes, and is
    119   basically a 3-part texture, but the omitted
    3 voices   voice constantly fluctuates. ISub.(4) is first stated in sequence in the B, continued in imitation between A and T. IISub.(3) is stated in inversion by A and T, and then in normal order by T and B. ISub.(3) is heard in sequence and imitation by S, A, and B, and then the voices return to IISub.(3). The last voices to remain silent in this episode are the T and A, leading to the statements of Sub. I by the T, and Sub. II by the A, in M. 119.

C.	EPISODE NO.	
No.	AND MEASURES	GENERAL DESCRIPTION

(IX) (8) Ms. 127–
130
4 voices

ISub.(4) stated by the T Sub. is imitated by the B and S. The B then imitates Motive (3) of the A Sub. II, in inversion. The remaining voices freely cadence.

Although Contrapunctus IX is written for 4 voices, the usage of 4 voices is relatively sparse. Even in the Expo., 4 voices are heard together only in Ms. 22–25, included with numerous rests. The Expo. does not end with 4 voices, so that the last statement of the Ans. concludes with 4 measures in 3 voices. A closer analysis of the measures with 4 continuous voices reveals a procedure of dynamic intensity in this fugue. Great care is taken to retain a 3-voice texture in the episodes in order to relieve the tension of the combination of the two subjects. Although numerous episodes have but one voice silent, Episode (7) shows the meticulous attention given to changing the strength of varying combinations of voices in contrasting ranges and motives. Care is deliberately taken to have the entrance of the 4th voice overlap with the remaining 3 voices in no longer duration than an eighth note.

The B has an unusually long period of silence from Ms. 36-1/2 to 58-1/2, which gives to this lengthy part a brighter texture until the B enters in M. 59-1/4. The T is then omitted so as to prevent the entrance of the B from becoming too strong dynamically.

X

The episodes and free material are closely integrated in this fugue.
OVERALL STRUCTURE: The 11 episodes occur primarily at the ends of the 2 expositions, at the ends of the 2 divisions, and after each stretto statement of the 2 subjects. The voice that is omitted prepares for the next entrance of a Sub. or Ans.

C.	EPISODE NO.	
No.	AND MEASURES	GENERAL DESCRIPTION

(X)   **(1)** Ms. 12 to 14-1/2 3 voices — T and B continue in imitation based on ISub. (2) and (3) in Expo. I. The S is basically free, with ISub.(3) heard in thirds with the B. A is silent.

(2) Ms. 18-23 basically 4 voices — All parts are freely based on Sub. I with the B partially sequential. The S continues with the first statement of Sub. II in Expo. II, after the ending of Div. One in M. 22-1/2.

(3) M. 30 2 voices — The S continues the free material from M. 29 in sequence. The T is freely based on Sub. I. The B and A remain silent.

(4) Ms. 38-44 3 voices

(4-A) 38-42 — The A, B, and S are individually sequential. The T is silent. M. 42 brings Div. Two to a close.

(4-B) 42-44 — The A is sequential; S and B are partially imitative. The T is silent.

(5) Ms. 47-1/2 to 52 3 then 4 voices — All voices are basically individually sequential. The delayed entrance of the S in M. 50-1/4 draws attention to the entrance of ISub.(2) on a weak beat of a measure, rather than on a strong beat as occurs in Sub. I. The S motive in M. 50-1/4 serves to imitate by inversion the preceding A usage of ISub.(2).

(6) Ms. 56-66 2 and 3 voices — This imitative episode can be compared to the intermediate episodes in Contrapunctus V. Here the episode is more extended, with ISub.(2) being the basis of the imitative passage. Each of the 4 voices states an extended version of ISub.(2), in a cycle of descending fifths:

T	starting on	"e"
S	"	on "a"
A	"	on "d"
B	"	on "g" .

Motive (2) starts on beat 2 for each successive entrance.

C.	EPISODE NO.	
No.	AND MEASURES	GENERAL DESCRIPTION

(X)   (7) Ms. 70-75   Each of the voices is basically sequential.
            4 voices   S and B become imitative, as the A and T
            with rests   become imitative. Motives from Subs. I
                       and II are used.

         (8) Ms. 79-85   The upper 3 voices imitate each other in
            3 voices   various combinations, combining motives
            with rests   of both subjects. The B is silent.

         (9) Ms. 89-103
           (9-A) 89-98   T and B begin in imitation, with A and S
            4 voices   continuing in inverted imitation of the
            with rests   same motive. The voices then continue to
            at the   vary combinations of imitative voices,
            beginning   resulting in some individual sequential
                       passages.
           (9-B) 98-103   The S is essentially sequential. A and T
            3 voices   are individually sequential based on
                       motives of Sub. II, and jointly imitative.
                       The B is silent.

        (10) Ms. 107-   ISub.(2) is the basic motive used and im-
             115   itated freely. The T has a series of
            3 voices   octave leaps in Ms. 110-111. The B is
                       silent.

        (11) Ms. 119-   The final two measures of the coda and the
             120   fugue gradually subside in rhythmic and
            4 voices   harmonic movement.

THE TWO TRIPLE FUGUES

VIII   OVERALL STRUCTURE: The episodes intricately
                               complete the three divisions; separate the
                               two-voice stretto statements in Secs. IV
                               and VI; and separate the three-voice
                               stretto statements or triple counterpoint
                               in Secs. VII and VIII. Individual voices
                               in sequence resulting in imitation in
                               pairs is frequently used.

         (1) Ms. 5 to   This brief passage in the A not only serves
            6-1/2   as the episode leading to the first Ans.
            1 voice   I, but also can be said to be the start
                      of the CS for Sub. I, since all statements
                      of Sub. I and Ans. I in the first Expo.
                      are followed by the beginning of this

C. No.	EPISODE NO. AND MEASURE	GENERAL DESCRIPTION
(VIII)	(1)	(cont.) episode. The first motive of this episode is used in sequence, the second statement of the motive being heard with the next statement of Ans. I or Sub. I.
	(2) Ms. 10 to 11-1/2 2 voices	The B has the episode and CS described in Episode (1). The A has free material.
	(3) Ms. 15 to 21-1/2 3 voices (3-A) 15-17	This section of Episode (3) completes Expo. I. All 3 voices are individually sequential. The S has Episode (1) and the beginning of the CS. The A and B state motives based on the CS, and their individual voices in sequence are stated in imitation.
	(3-B) 17 to 21-1/2	The B motives in M. 17 with pedal point "d" in M. 18 are imitated first by the S and then the A, and back to the B. The rest of the material is free. The S and A cadence at M. 21-1/2, preparing the A Ans. I in M. 21-1/2 and the S obbligato-like passage above it.
	(4) Ms. 25 to 35-1/2 3 voices (4-A) 25-31	All 3 voices basically proceed by individual sequence, based on motives from either Sub. I or its CS, as found in Expo. I, resulting in imitative passages in varying combinations.
	(4-B) 31 to 35-1/2	While the basic procedure is followed as described in Episode (4-A), the 2-measure pedal point in the B in Ms. 31-32 gives a temporary cadential implication before continuing, so as to prepare for the entrance of the B Sub. I in M. 35-1/2. The entire Episode (4) is the last episode and the longest in Division One emphasizing Sub. I.

C.	EPISODE NO.	
No.	AND MEASURES	GENERAL DESCRIPTION

(VIII)

(5) Ms. 47(1/2) to 49-1/2
3 voices

All 3 voices are basically individually sequential, with the motives being based on the end of the preceding stretto statements of Sub. I and Ans. II. Some imitation results between S and A.

(6) Ms. 53 to 61-1/2
3 voices

(6-A) 53-4

The 3 voices imitate the preceding Sec. and bring Expo. II to a close.

(6-B) 54 to 61-1/2

The 3 voices proceed by various imitative devices, including mirror imitation between the S and B in M. 57. Although the 3 voices are based on motives from Subs. I and II and CS I, there is some new material, as found in the S in Ms. 58-3/4 to 60. This last S passage can be viewed as anticipating Sub. III, but in augmentation and with a syncopated shift in rhythm.

(7) Ms. 65 to 67-3/4
3 voices

The B begins by proceeding by sequence with motives presented in the last measure of the preceding Sec. The A imitates the B in mirror imitation in M. 65. The S then imitates by mirror imitation the continuous sequential pattern of the B in M. 66. The A is both imitative and sequential.

(8) Ms. 71 to 81-3/4
3 voices

Whereas the sections emphasizing Sub. I had one lengthy episode, Episode (4), Div. Two has 2 lengthy episodes, Episodes (8) and (9). Episode (8) is the longest, and has similar procedures as the preceding episodes, but motives from Sub. II are included in sequence and imitation between the voices. Two false entrances of Sub. II exist.

(9) Ms. 85 to 94-1/4
3 voices

This episode is more climactic than Episode (8) because it is the last episode leading to the end of Div. Two. While imitation and sequence based on motives similar to Episode (8) are present, additional climactic elements exist in Episode (9).

(9-A) 85 to 93-1/2

Rests and quarter notes over the measure in the A in Ms. 87 and 88 create a chordal texture implying finality. The close

313

C. No.	EPISODE NO. AND MEASURES	GENERAL DESCRIPTION
(VIII)	(9-A)	(cont.) imitation of the S and A in Ms. 88-1/2 to 91 based on motives from Sub. II convey paired movement in the 2 voices, resulting in emphasis on the upper voices, the voices being in a fairly high range. The B during this passage proceeds in quarter-note movement as a supporting voice to the S and A. Ms. 90-3/4 to 93-1/2 use 16th-note and 32nd-note movement for rhythmic cadential emphasis. These faster notes are used later in the fugue with the same climactic function.
	(9-B) 93-1/2 to 94-1/4 2 voices	This brief passage introduces the initial entry of Sub. III. The B is imitated by the S in inversion.
	(10) Ms. 98 to 99-1/4 3 voices	This partially-imitative episode is a brief transitional passage leading to the next statement by the B of Ans. III.
	(11) Ms. 103 to 105-1/4 3 voices with rests	The S imitates the A by inversion. The A then imitates the same inverted order of the S. A usage of larger intervallic skips for emphasis is found in M. 104 in the B. Although the S is silent for 3 beats, the B has larger intervals on beat 2, which gradually get smaller in size leading to the entrance of Sub. III by the S in M. 105-1/4.
	(12) Ms. 109 to 125-1/2	This lengthy episode serves many functions. It concludes the fughetta for Sub. III, M. 124-1/2.
	(12-A) 109 to 117-1/4 3 voices	Ms. 109-111 conclude the basic presentation of the 3 voices for Expo III ending in a deceptive cadence to the subdominant of D Minor. The voices are imitative. In Ms. 111 to 114, all 3 voices are in constant movement, with numerous chromatically-altered harmonies. Ms. 114 to 117-1/4 resolve the tension of these chromatic and rhythmically-dense harmonies, by having the 2 upper voices proceed over a pedal point in the B. This passage gives the impression of a fugal ending. The S has the greatest movement, stating consistent motives from Sub. III in sequence. The A is sequential based on the 1st motive of Sub. I

C.	EPISODE NO.	
No.	AND MEASURES	GENERAL DESCRIPTION

(VIII)

(12-B) 117-1/4
to 124-1/2
3 voices

By imitation between voices and then paired, based on motives in sequence primarily from Sub. II, and by 16th-note motives, this passage can be equated to a codetta or coda. Div. Three includes Expo. III, versatile Episode (12), and ends with a lengthy pedal point and codetta, ending in A Minor.

(12-C) 124-1/2
to 125-1/2
1 and 2
voices

This brief passage introduces the first of 2 final stretto statements of Subs. I and II before the three-voice stretto passages begin. The S Sub. imitates the B motives taken from Sub. II. The A is silent.

(13) Ms. 129
to 131-1/2
2 voices

The S and A proceed by individual sequential passages. The B is silent.

(14) Ms. 135
to 147-1/2
(148)
3 voices
with rests

This is the last episode before the start of the statements of the 3 subjects in triple counterpoint. A constant labyrinth of imitative passages occurs based essentially on the free material presented by the S in Sec. VIB. Mirror imitation, paired voices in imitation, imitation by inversion, are all part of the imitative procedures. A succession of transient modulations pass through the keys of A Minor, G Minor, C Major, F Major, D Minor, and back to A Minor leading to the entry of the three-voice stretto in Ms. 147 and 148. The S remains silent in Ms. 145-1/4 to 147-1/2.

(15) Ms. 152
to 152-1/2
2 voices

This brief passage is transitional to the next triple counterpoint statement. The motives are based on Subs. I and III.

(16) Ms. 156
to 158-3/4
3 voices

This passage is transitional to the next three-voice stretto section. An unexpected procedure appears. The A and B are heard in parallel 3rds and 6ths descending in quarter-note movement in M. 157. This is followed by descending parallel 3rds (10ths) in S and A in M. 158 in 8th notes. Imitation in pairs in dimunution is the result.

315

C. No.	EPISODE NO. AND MEASURES	GENERAL DESCRIPTION

(VIII)

(17) Ms. 163
to 170-1/2
3 voices

The passage is basically imitative and sequential, ending with 2 measures over a pedal point in Ms. 168-169. The voices are predominantly individually sequential. Motives from Sub. II are emphasized in the passage directly proceeding to the next triple statement.

(18) Ms. 175
to 182
3 voices

(18-A) 175
to 180

The first part of Episode (18) concludes the four triple statements of the three subjects. Following imitation between the voices based on the free material in the preceding Sec., 16th-note movement in the S accompanied by paired voices in chordal style based on figures from Sub. II bring Sec. VII to a close.

(18-B) 180
to 182

However, the episode continues, and this part of the episode initiates the coda. The motives of Sub. II are stated in imitation above a pedal point in the B.

(19) Ms. 187
to 188
3 voices

Following a pedal point in the S in M. 186, the S continues with one last 16th-note passage in M. 187, and all voices gradually resolve their rhythmic and motivic interest.

XI

OVERALL STRUCUTURE: Despite the brevity of the episodes in this fugue, the episodes take on the characteristics of the sections surrounding them, and thereby add significantly to the contrapuntal procedures of this fugue.

(1) Ms. 17-22

(1-A) 17 to
18-1/2
4 voices

This brief episode serves to conclude Expo. I with no new material presented. The last B figure in M. 17 taken from Sub. I is imitated by the S and A in M. 18 in mirror imitation.

(1-B) 18-1/4
to 22
3 and 4
voices

This same figure from Sub. I is imitated by all voices, combining 3 voices in M. 21 in parallel movement. The A is sequential in Ms. 19-3/4 to 22.

C.	EPISODE NO.	
No.	AND MEASURES	GENERAL DESCRIPTION

(XI)

(2) Ms. 26 to 27-1/2 4 voices

The Chr. M. which plays such a large role in Div. Two is stated in its entirety in the A in Ms. 25-1/4 to 26-1/2, in inverted order, partially heard in stretto with the end of Sub. 1 in M. 25. This brief episode completes Div. One.

(3) Ms. 31 to 34-1/2 3 voices, then 2 voices

Episodes (3) to (6) occur between each statement of Sub. II or Ans. II in Expo. II. The Chr. M. heard in Episode (2) is stated again in the A in this episode. Since it is the lower voice in a 2-part structure with S and A, the harmony is considerably colored. The S then continues an ascending chromatic figure in M. 34 in imitation by inversion. The S proceeds by sequence above the Chr. M. in the A before stating its chromatic figure.

(4) Ms. 38-44 basically 3 voices

The last motive of Sub. II, plus the Chr. M., serve as the bases for the motivic sequences and passages in imitation in this episode. The S and A continue in constant movement, while the T and B alternate and imitate each other separated by rests. The T has a 2-measure rest before its entrance in normal order of the Chr. M. in M. 44-1/4.

(5) Ms. 47-57 basically 4 voices

This is the longest episode in Expo. II. The 4 voices are essentially individually sequential, forming varying combinations of imitative voices. Figures are taken from the Chr. M., and motives are taken from Subs. I and II. A complete inverted statement of the Chr. M. starting on the dominant of D Minor is stated by the S in Ms. 54-1/4 to 56, imitated in stretto and inversion by the B in Ms. 55-1/4 to 57.

(6) Ms. 60 to 67-3/4
  (6-A) 60 to 61-1/4 4 voices

This brief episode completes Expo. II, ending in C Major.

  (6-B) 61-1/4 to 67-3/4 basically

This is the last episode before one last statement of Sub. II in normal order by the B, to end Div. Two. Motives from Sub. II

317

(XI) (6-B)   and figures from the Chr. M. are the
        4 voices   bases for the imitation and sequential
                           passages. A descending chromatic scale in
                           the T using 10 notes begins in M. 64-1/4
                           and continues constantly by various sus-
                           pensions to M. 67-1/2, leading directly to
                           Ans. II in the B. The S continues the Chr.
                           M. in stretto with the B Ans. II. Episode
                           (6-B), plus the 3 voices above the Ans. II
                           by the B in Sec. IV are all highly chro-
                           matic. Chromaticism appropriately ends Div.
                           Two for emphasis, since the Chr. M. was so
                           significant in this division.

      (7) Ms. 75 to   Episode (7) is transitional, continuing the
          76-1/4   motives of the preceding section.
          4 voices

      (8) Ms. 88 to   This brief passage brings Div. Three to a
          89-1/2   close in F Major.
          4 voices

      (9) Ms. 93-1/4   This episode separates imitatively Sec. VIA
          to 93-3/4   from VIB.
          3 voices

     (10) Ms. 97-   Motives from Sub. III are begun by the S,
          100   and imitated first by the A and then T,
          4 voices   leading by imitation to the next statement
                           of Sub. III by the B in M. 100-1/4. The B
                           entrance of Sub. III is preceded by a one-
                           measure pedal point in the B in M. 99, over
                           which all 3 voices state some form of mo-
                           tives of Sub. III in stretto. The main
                           motives of Sub. III in this episode are in
                           normal order, as is the next statement of
                           Sub. III by the B.

     (11) Ms. 109   Motives from Sub. III are begun by the A,
          to 111-3/4   and imitated first by the S and then by the
          3 voices   T. All motives from Sub. III are in normal
                           order, as were the 2 preceding statements
                           of Sub. III. The B is silent, leading to
                           the false entry of the B Sub. III in the
                           next Intermediate Section (A).

     (12) Ms. 124-1/2   These 2 beats briefly separate by paired
          to 125   voices the 2 retrograde stretto statements

318

C. No.	EPISODE NO. AND MEASURES	GENERAL DESCRIPTION

(XI)

(12)
2 beats
4 voices

of Sub. III from the 2 normal stretto statements of the same Sub.

(13) Ms. 128-
130
4 voices

This episode brings to a conclusion the stretto statements of Sub. III in Sec. VII. The ending pedal point in the B gives an area of relaxation before the quadruple brief statements in Intermediate Section (B).

(14) Ms. 136
to 136-3/4
4 voices

These 3 beats separate Sec. VIII from the triple statements of the subjects in Sec. IX.

(15) Ms. 144-
146
4 then 3
voices

Reduced rhythmic and melodic movement create some relaxation following Intermediate Section (C), bringing this intermediate section to a close, and leading to the next triple counterpoint Sec. X. The T becomes silent.

(16) Ms. 150-1/4
to 152-3/4
3 voices

Starting in M. 149-1/2, the S states motives from Sub. III in normal order, imitated in turn by the A, T, and B, all in normal order. The lower of the next 2 mirror statements of Sub. III is in normal order. The silent voice constantly changes with the changing imitation.

(17) Ms. 155-
158
4 voices

The upper 3 voices state constantly changing motives based on Sub. III in a heightened climactic section, over a descending Chr. M. extended to an 11-note chromatic scale.

(18) Ms. 162-1/4
to 164-1/4
4 voices
with numer-
ous tied
notes

A brief figure from Sub. III is imitated in the upper 3 voices, after tied half-notes, reducing to some degree the tension of the 2nd mirror stretto statement, before proceeding to the 3rd mirror statement in M. 164-1/4. The B continues with the Chr. M. as was done in Episode (17), but in this Episode (18) the Chr. M. is fragmented and abbreviated.

(19) Ms. 172-1/2
to 175

Less rhythmic activity, less melodic movement, and less chromaticism permit this

319

(XI)

(19)
      4 voices   episode to resolve the tension before the
final 2 triple statements of the subjects
in the coda. Melodic attention is directed
to the highest voice, the S, in high regis-
ter.

(20) Ms. 179   This brief episode separates the 2 triple
    to 179-3/4 statements of the subjects in the coda. The
    4 voices   outer voices continue motives begun in the
preceding Sec. XIIA.

THE TWO MIRROR FUGUES: Despite the considerations
for the inverted voices for the mirror fugues, the
episodes and free material can offer new insights for
contrapuntal procedures.

XVI
      OVERALL STRUCTURE: The 5 episodes in this
fugue are included between each of the 5
sections and after the coda. Although the
episodes show a close integration to the
major sections, each episode shows a continuous expansion of one contrapuntal idea.
Lengthy rests in any one voice are planned
to anticipate the next entrance in the same
voice of the Sub. or Ans. Pedal points are
strategically added in sequence progressing
from voice to voice. The descriptions given
are for the rectus setting of Contrapunctus
XVI; the inversus setting would have changes
in voice and key.

(1) Ms. 13-20   The B imitates the last measure of the S
    3 then 2   Sub. in normal and inverted orders, while
    voices   the A continues in sequence the motive
presented in the A in the penultimate measure of the Expo. The S and A progress as a
duo over the moving B, with the A remaining
silent after M. 16-1/2.

(2) Ms. 24-29   The S and A alternate the last motive of the
    3 voices   A Ans. in M. 23, with the parts interchanged
    with rests, and the motives inverted. The B quarter
    then 2   notes over the bar-lines most frequently are

C.	EPISODE NO.	
No.	AND MEASURES	GENERAL DESCRIPTION

(XVI)

    (2)

        voices — for roots of the chords in the rectus setting.

    (3) Ms. 41-48
        3 voices — The alternations between the S and A are exchanged and inverted.

    (4) Ms. 52-62
        3 voices — Melodic additions in the B are present, and the B emphasizes chords over the bar-lines. The S now takes over the rests included in the B in Episode (3). The S "b-flat" sustained by a fermata in M. 59 goes up rather than down as in the inversus setting.

    (5) Ms. 70-71
        3 voices — The final 2 measures bring the coda to a close.

XVII — OVERALL STRUCTURE: Following one short episode in the Expo., episodes occur at the end of the Expo. and after each statement of the Sub. While the episodes are basically transitional, they help to establish the ultimate 8th-note movement of this fugue. Starting with a sparing use of 8th notes in the B in M. 8, the 8th-note movement becomes so consistent that by M. 31, 8th notes become the basic background and movement. The 7 episodes and the free material show a close motivic relationship to the Sub. and its elaborated versions in this fugue. Because of gradual increased 8th-note movement, by the time M. 21 states the elaborated version of the Sub., it is completely prepared. The individual voices in the episodes are basically sequential and imitative. The descriptions given are for the rectus setting of Contrapunctus XVII; the inversus setting would have changes in voice and key.

    (1) Ms. 9-1/4
        to 10
        3 beats,
        2 voices — Both voices proceed individually in sequence as a transition to the next entrance of the A Sub. in M. 10.

    (2) Ms. 18-21
        4 voices — The individual voices are basically sequential, following motives in M. 17, the penultimate measure of the Expo. The S

(XVII)

    (2)   (cont.) and A proceed in pairs, with the
                                       B and T being somewhat imitative.

    (3) Ms. 25-1/4   The measure is partly imitative and serves
        to 26   as a transition to the next entrance of the
        4 voices   A Sub. in M. 26.

    (4) Ms. 30-32   The A is sequential based on the motive in
        3 voices   the penultimate measure of the A Sub.
                   directly preceding it. The B proceeds by
                   sequence based on free material, while the S
                   is free. The T is silent.

    (5) Ms. 36-42   This is the longest episode. Almost a
        3 voices   consistent 8th-note movement takes place.
                   The S and A are free, and proceed together
                   with some imitation. The T is sequential.
                   The B is omitted.

    (6) Ms. 46-50   The B is partially sequential, but otherwise
        4 voices   the voices are free. Imitation exists
        with some   mainly between the outer voices. An 8th-
        rests   note movement is consistent, with two 16th
                   notes in the S at the end of M. 49.

    (7) CODA,   The coda continues the 8th-note movement
        Ms. 54-56   between the 4 voices over a final pedal-
        4 voices   point in the B. The rhythm becomes more
                   complex, with the upper 2 voices moving in
                   pairs. The T has an extended 8th-note
                   passage with two 16th notes at the end of
                   M. 55. The B ends the rhythmic interest of
                   the coda with a 16th-note figure extending
                   the final D Major chord to M. 56-1/2. The
                   B figure is ideally suited for the S in the
                   inversion of this fugue.

XVIII   THE QUADRUPLE FUGUE

                   OVERALL STRUCTURE: The episodes reveal a
                   constant overlapping of cadence endings in
                   transient modulations, leading directly to
                   new Sub. and Ans. statements. The episodes
                   are closely integrated to the free material.

    (1) Ms. 29-1/2   This brief passage serves as a transition
        to 30-1/2   between Secs. IIA and IIB, continuing in

(XVIII)

(1)
       4 voices   (cont.) sequence the motives preceding it.

(2) Ms. 35-1/2   A cadential implication in D Minor is heard
    to 37-1/2   before proceeding to the next stretto in
    4 voices   Sec. IIC.

(3) M. 43-1/4   This 1 beat separates the stretto statement
    1 beat   from the next Sec. III, and the A is part of
    4 voices   a motive imitating the S in M. 42. M. 43
               has a cadential implication to C Major.

(4) Ms. 48-1/4   The A melodic line begun in M. 46-1/4 is
    to 55-1/2   imitated by the S in M. 47-1/4, and these
    3 voices   voices continue in imitation to M. 50. The
               2 voices continue partially imitative,
               joining together in parallel 6ths in M. 55
               (to M. 60). The B proceeds by sequence in
               constant quarter-note movement. The T
               remains silent.

(5) Ms. 60-1/2   The T in M. 60-3/4 imitates the A from M.
    to 61-1/2   59-3/4, which is brought to partial cadential
    3 voices   conclusion. The B is briefly silent.

(6) Ms. 67-1/2   By partial cadential implication, the 2
    to 71   stretto statements in Sec. IV are separated.
    4 voices

(7) Ms. 77-1/2   This episode has a false entry of Ans. I
    to 81-1/2   inverted presented in the S in M. 79-1/2
    4 voices   and concluding in M. 84. The B is partially
               sequential.

(8) Ms. 86-1/2   The 3 upper voices alternate motives in
    to 89-1/2   imitation. The B remains silent.
    3 voices

(9) Ms. 104-1/4   Partially imitative and by tied whole notes,
    to 105-3/4   this episode temporarily relaxes the 2 stret-
    4 voices   to statements in Sec. VI before the final
               statement by the B of Sub. I in Sec. VII at
               the end of Div. One.

(10) Ms. 110-1/2 The first fughetta in Div. One is concluded
    to 115   over 4 measures of pedal point in the B.
    4 voices   The parts have some imitation, but are

C.	EPISODE NO.	
No.	AND MEASURES	GENERAL DESCRIPTION

(XVIII)

(10)   (cont.) basically free with considerable large intervallic skips. The S ends on "3-natural" in D Minor, which was the starting note of the new Sub. II in the A in M. 114-1/4.

(11) Ms. 127-1/4   This is the only episode in Expo. II. It
     to 128-1/4   separates the first 2 statements of Sub. II
     2 voices   and Ans. II from the second 2 statements.
The S continues by sequence its motive in M. 126. The A has an ascending partially-chromatic scale leading back to D.Minor.

(12) Ms. 141-1/4   Although this lengthy episode does not end
     to 147-1/4   Expo. II proper, it does serve to conclude
     3 voices   the section stating Sub. II by itself.
     briefly,   After this episode with rather a clearly-
     then   defined cadence in D Minor in M. 147(-1/4),
     4 voices   Sub. II proceeds in two-voice or three-voice stretto in its fughetta. The motive taken from Sub. II and presented by the B in M. 141 is in turn imitated by all the voices. The S is sequential, and creates imitation with contrasting voices.

(13) Ms. 154-1/4   The voices imitate in turn the last motive
     to 156-1/4   of Sub. II. The A is silent.
     2 voices and
     3 voices

(14) Ms. 162-1/4   The A and T imitate each other, based on
     to 167-1/4   the last motive of the A Ans. II in M. 161
     3 voices,   and leading directly to the next Sub. II
     then   stated by the T. The B proceeds by se-
     2 voices   quence. The S is silent.

(15) Ms. 174-1/2   The voices imitate each other based on
     to 180-1/4   small figures from the last motive of Sub.
     4 voices   II. The figures are presented in normal and inverted orders. The last motive of Sub. II is then stated in its entirety in imitation. The B is briefly silent.

(16) Ms. 188-1/2   This episode ends the fughetta in Div.
     to 193-1/4   Two in G Minor. Imitation is based on
     4 voices   motives and figures from the last motive of
     with rests   Sub. II. The free material is cadential

(XVIII)
         (16)   in intent.

         (17) Ms. 199-1/4 The T followed by the A proceed by con-
              to 201-1/2   tinuous imitation leading to the next state-
              2 voices   ment of Sub. III in the S in M. 201-1/2.

         (18) Ms. 205-1/4
              to 210-1/2
           (18-A) 205-1/4 Proceeding by imitation of preceding mo-
              to 207-1/4   tives, Expo. III is brought to a conclusion
                           in A Minor.
           (18-B) 207-1/4 The 3 voices continue in imitation with
              to 210-1/2   each other, starting with the S motive in
              3 voices   M. 205-3/4. The A, then B, imitate this
                           same motive. The cadence at the end of
                           Expo. III overlaps with Episode (18-B).

         (19) Ms. 216 to The start of this episode has a colorful
              217-1/2   harmonic usage of the Neapolitan sixth
              4 voices   chord in D Minor (in M. 215), which chord
                           is used to harmonize the inverted state-
                           ment of Sub. III transposed: "E-natural, F,
                           D, E-flat", for the last note "E-flat". The
                           2 lower voices and the S are individually
                           sequential, while the A has the customary
                           figure, now inverted, following the state-
                           ment of Sub. III.

         (20) Ms. 230-   This episode concludes Div. Three. It ends
              233   on the dominant of D Minor, which climac-
              4 voices   tically leads to the incomplete statement
                           of the three subjects in Sec. XIV. A lilt-
                           ing 16th-note figure adds rhythmic momen-
                           tum to the cadence. A brief pedal point
                           exists in the B in M. 230. The 4 voices
                           are widely spaced for added sonority. The
                           voices are partially imitative and sequen-
                           tial, with 2 beats of mirror imitation be-
                           tween the S and B in M. 230 and 231-1/2, with
                           both voices being given the lilting 16th-
                           note figure. The T has rather large inter-
                           vals in M. 230 between the pedal point in
                           the B, and paired voices in parallel 3rds
                           above it. The free material adds cadential
                           and climactic intent.

325

THE CODAS:

The coda can serve as a summation of musical ideas;
an expanded recapitulation of the ideas presented in the
exposition; or a few measures to relax the tension. Any
of these goals need not be restricted to a fugue type.

Although the within analysis of the codas refers
to the final coda only, in the fugues with more than one
subject, contrasts of ideas could be present if a fugue
has more than one coda, especially if one or more subjects is presented in its own fughetta.

THE CODAS

CONTRAPUNCTUS NO.	SUB. OR ANS. PRESENT	FINAL CADENCE	SPECIAL ATTRIBUTES
THE FOUR SIMPLE FUGUES			
I Ms. 74-78	Ans. by T	plagal, d	In keeping with the original tight entrances of the Sub. and Ans. in the Expo., the material for the coda requires no more time than is required for one final statement of the Ans. The pedal point is longer than the pedal point in Episode (6) for added finality.
II Ms. 79-84	Sub. by S	plagal, d	The S was the last voice of the Expo., and states the Sub. in the coda. The coda ends with an episode, as did the Expo. The subdominant begins the coda, and is heard in the last 3 measures.
III Ms. 70-72	None	plagal, d	The brief coda continues the short imitative passages of Episode (8-A), with a gradual reduction in rhythmic and melodic interest. The T and A extend the cadence in M. 72, which 2 voices began this fugue. The subdominant is emphasized.
IV Ms. 129-138	Sub. modified by T; then Sub. by A	d minor	When the T states modified Sub., no CS is included; the T has reference to CS when A states Sub. The B begins with 1 measure pedal point to emphasize the beginning of the coda, stating the tonic of G minor. The B then continues partially sequential with unusually large intervals in its motives. The S and A are freely paired. Beginning with M. 132-1/2 the S imitates the motives previously stated by the B in Ms. 130 and 131. From M. 134 S and T are paired, first in mirror imitation, then in rhythmic imitation. The B has a lengthy pedal point beginning in M. 135 to the end. Phrases constantly overlap in this coda, obscuring

THE CODAS (continued)

CONTRAPUNCTUS NO.	SUB. OR ANS. PRESENT	FINAL CADENCE	SPECIAL ATTRIBUTES
(IV)			the clearly-defined nature of the Sub. statements. This device might have been used to anticipate the next group of stretto fugues. Large and exaggerated skips are heard in voices other than the Sub. The rhythmic imitation in the S and T in Ms. 135 to 136-1/2 can be compared to CS(1) in Contrapunctus I. The T in Ms. 136-1/2 to 137 can be compared to the first part of the CS in Contrapunctus III. These references may have been planned as an appropriate conclusion to the 4 simple fugues.
THE THREE STRETTO FUGUES			
V Ms. 86-90	Ans., normal, by A Sub., inverted, by B I	d minor	The final 2 statements are heard simultaneously in mirror stretto. The conclusion of the mirror stretto coincides with the end of this stretto fugue. A 5th voice as Bass II is added throughout the coda below the Sub. presented by B I. A 6th voice as Soprano II is added in M. 88-3/4. The resulting 6 parts create a dense harmonic sonority to conclude the six-sectional fugue. The entrance of the A Ans. in M. 86 is disguised by an ornamented resolution of the suspension at the conclusion of Sec. V. This disguised entrance permits B I to be heard as Sub. before the A joins audibly as Ans. in mirror stretto. The A and B began the Expo., but the statements of both voices are reversed in the coda.
VI Ms. 74-1/2 to 79	Sub., normal, by T, dim, Ans., inverted, by S, normal note values	d minor	The order of the 3 voices in the coda reflects the change in emphasis from the first division to the second:

328

THE CODAS (continued)

CONTRAPUNCTUS NO.	SUB. OR ANS. PRESENT	FINAL CADENCE	SPECIAL ATTRIBUTES
(VI)	Sub., normal, by A, dim.		See below
VII Ms. 60-61	None	d minor	See below

SPECIAL ATTRIBUTES

	In Exposition I		In the Coda	
Ms. 1-5	B' S normal		Ms. 74-1/2 to T S normal, 76-1/2 dim.	
Ms. 2-4	S A inverted, dim.		Ms. 75-1/2 to S A inverted 79 dim.	
Ms. 3-1/2 A to 5-1/2	S normal, dim.		Ms. 76-1/2 to A S normal, 78-1/2 dim.	

The entire coda has a "d" pedal point in the B. The harmony is unusual in that the entire coda is in G minor, with the exception of the last 2 chords. The last 2 chords do not give a feeling of finality, since the first of the 2 chords has a 16th-note duration with the chord of A Major, and the last chord ends with the 3rd in the S, in D Major. The voice parts in the last 2 chords are expanded to 7 parts. The entrances of the 3 voices stating Sub. and Ans. in the coda anticipate the entrances of the first 3 statements in the Expo. of Contrapunctus VII. In the coda of C. VI, each voice enters after 1 measure, and all voices begin on the 3rd beat of each measure. In the Expo. of C. VII, each voice enters after 1 measure, but all voices begin on the 1st beat of each measure. The A entrance in M. 3 of C. VII inverts the Sub., but otherwise the 2 schemes are identical.

Following an intensely-complex fugal structure with very short episodes, and following a highly chromatic harmonic texture in Episode (4-A), this brief coda serves to resolve the tension. Chromatic half-steps occur between motives; imitation between voices takes place; and the B has a pedal point for 1-1/2 measures.

329

THE CODAS (continued)

CONTRAPUNCTUS NO.	SUB. OR ANS. PRESENT	FINAL CADENCE	SPECIAL ATTRIBUTES
THE TWO DOUBLE FUGUES			
IX Ms. 119-130	Sub. I by T Sub. II by A	d minor	The coda has one final statement of both Subjects I and II. The entrance of the voices in Sec. IV is the reverse of Sec. III. The final A and T began and ended Expo. I. Sub. I is above Sub. I, as is found at the beginning of Sec. II when the subjects are first combined. The coda has a brief concluding episode in Ms. 127-130.
X Ms. 115-120	Sub. I by A and T in 3rds Sub. II by B	d minor	The last three-voice stretto is stated in the coda. The first 3 voices to enter in Expo. I are combined for this last stretto statement. The B statement of Sub. II is the same as the initial statement of Sub. II by the S in Expo. II, with the exception of the last few notes. The A Sub. I is the same as the first A Sub. I in the opening Expo., with the exception of the last note as "f-natural". The T states Sub. I in parallel 3rds with the A. The suspension in the cadence in M. 120 is similar to the cadence ending in M. 22-1/4 at the end of Div. One. Two statements of Sub. I are heard above one statement of Sub. II. A 2-measure episode concludes the coda.
THE TWO TRIPLE FUGUES			
VIII Ms. 180-188	Sub. I. normal, S Sub. II, normal, A Sub. III, inverted, B	d minor	The 3 subjects in triple counterpoint are the same as the initial statements in each of the 3 expositions, with the two exceptions of the second note of Sub. I in M. 183 in the S, and the "e-flat" for the last motive of Sub. II. These 3 subjects had been stated together in Sec. VIIC, all real, in the key of the subdominant, G Minor. Greater 16th-note movement exists in the brief episode at the end of the coda. The usage of 16th-note movement for emphasis was seen in the codetta at the end of Expo. III; in Ms. 178-179 leading

330

THE CODAS (continued)

CONTRAPUNCTUS NO.	SUB. OR ANS. PRESENT	FINAL CADENCE	SPECIAL ATTRIBUTES
(VIII)			to the start of the coda in M. 180; and in a few other minor climaxes as in Ms. 120-121. The 16th-note movement in Ms. 178-179 leading to the coda is especially climactic because the notes occur in the S in a wide and high range.
XI Ms. 174-3/4 to 184	Sub. II, inverted, B Sub. III, retro-grade, T Sub. I, normal, A Sub. III, retro-grade, B Sub. II, inverted, T Sub. I, normal, S	d minor	Beginning on a deceptive cadence, two triple statements of the 3 subjects occur in D Minor in varying combinations. The 3 subjects are basically the same as the first statements of the subjects in their respective expositions. The free material is based on motives from the 3 subjects. A 5th voice is added with the S in M. 183. Sub. I begins in the T in the first triple statement of the subjects in Sec. X; Sub. I then moves to the A as the upper voice in the first triple state-ment in the coda; Sub. I ultimately progresses to the S in a relatively high register for the final triple statement of the coda. Following this procedure, Sub. II begins in the S, moves to the B, and ends in the T or mid-voice. Sub. III begins in the A, moves to the T, and ends in the B, or lowest voice. A brief episode occurs between the two triple state-ments in the coda, with no episode at the conclusion of the fugue.

THE TWO MIRROR FUGUES

CONTRAPUNCTUS NO.	SUB. OR ANS. PRESENT	FINAL CADENCE	SPECIAL ATTRIBUTES
XVI Ms. 62-71	Sub. by B Ans. by S	d minor	The last 2 voices of the Expo., the B and S, conclude the coda, but interchange the fugue statements. Both statements of the Sub. and Ans. are identical to those stated in the Expo. Three successive pedal points are significant in the coda. A brief episode is added at the end.
XVII Ms. 54-56	None	d minor	This brief concluding coda is described under Episode (7).

CHAPTER FIVE
CONCLUSIONS

Die Kunst der Fuge continues to guide composers and theorists in fugal construction. Basic fugue types and structures open doors to numerous other fugue schemes. This "Thesaurus of Fugal Writing", as Die Kunst der Fuge could be called, lays the groundwork for an unlimited supply of fugal procedures. Hundreds of fugues in the higher levels of stretto, double, triple, quadruple, mirror, and canonic fugues, could be written as a result of a careful analysis of this work. Regardless of the harmonic idiom, the fugal structures in Die Kunst der Fuge could inexhaustibly furnish resources for new fugue compositions.

The summations presented in this chapter give some concept of the wealth of fugal insights contained in Die Kunst der Fuge based on the studies made within this thesis.

THE FUGUE TYPES

Bach used the leading fugue types in existence in the Baroque era to complete Die Kunst der Fuge to illustrate his concepts in this additive study. This work could have been extended with additional fugues, if new and innovative fugue types or procedures were intended to be part of this study.

THE OVERALL STRUCTURES

Bach not only planned the orders of subjects and answers following the expositions to appear in subsequent keys or with modified entries, but devised a skeletal outline around which the fabric of the fugue was spun. A cardinal example of an initial basic thematic outline is seen from a careful study of stretto fugue Contrapunctus VII.

After diagramming the subjects and answers in stretto combinations, Bach proceeded to add the episodes and contrapuntal free material in this fugue, as in the other fugues. In Contrapunctus VII, Bach logically includes episodes between statements of the augmented subject. The episodes could have been longer, especially Episode (2), which separates the two first statements of the subject in augmentation from the second two statements. A closer motivic relationship could have existed between Episodes (2) and (4).

In the same Contrapunctus VII, the continuous sixteenth note movement in the bass serves as a natural musical addition below the three voices in continuous stretto in Ms. 36 to 41. The inclusion of the bass movement at this juncture in the fugue could have resulted from Bach's study of the thematic outline. The new material throughout the fugue adds climax on strategic beats.

Contrapunctus VI serves as an example of the added material to the thematic outline taking on an individual dimension. Although the French rhythmic thrust is intimated in the statement of the subject in diminution, the real content of the French style is preserved for the episodes, free material, and new material.

The double and triple fugues give special attention in the basic thematic outline to the double and triple counterpoint statements of the two and three subjects in varying combinations. The episodes are added to the thematic outline in a way that the usage of smaller motives from the two or three subjects permits symmetrical planning.

Mirror Fugue Contrapunctus XVII divulges organized relationship of episodes around the three varied statements of the main subject.

THE SUBJECT

After a study of the variant statements of the subject in Die Kunst der Fuge has been made, it becomes visible that Bach gave consideration to the entire work when he first drafted his seemingly simple original subject. The following conclusions can be drawn regarding this subject:

1) The intervals in the original subject, together with the inversions of each motive, embody all the basic intervals for contrapuntal usage. This embodiment of the main intervals in the subject permits a close association between the motives of the episodes and the subject;

2) The original subject was designed so that it could be stated in stretto in an infinite number of combinations with itself with normal note values, in diminution, and in augmentation. A study of the basic thematic outlines of the stretto fugues on the motivic scores will show the many combinations which are possible;

3) The new subjects presented in the double and triple fugues not only embody the original subject in their melodic structure, but are contrived to combine with the original subject in singular ways:

a) The lengthy subject of double fugue Contrapunctus IX is combined with the augmented statement of the original subject in invertible counterpoint;

b) Double fugue Contrapunctus X as a stretto fugue combines with the stretto fugue subject in invertible counterpoint, with both subjects individually being stated in parallel thirds;

c) Not only do the three subjects in the triple fugues include the main notes of the original subject, but they combine with each other in invertible counterpoint, in either three- or four-part fugues.

4) The metric and rhythmic changes in a subject can produce different characteristics in the overall fugue. The overall style in a number of fugues in Die Kunst der Fuge could have been changed by the corresponding characteristic change in the fugue subject;

5) Any subject could have been used within one of the other fugue structures or fugue types, with varying procedural results;

6) The subject can be varied when it appears in later sections of the same fugue, as in mirror fugue Contrapunctus XVII;

7) A subject can be expanded by changing the meter and rhythm, and adding notes between the main beats, as in the subjects for the canons. In Contrapunctus XII, XIII, and XV, notes are added in varying ways around the original subject, from notes surrounding main beats to first beats in each measure (C. XIII), and to syncopated additions (C. XV);

8) Any of the canonic subjects could have been used for three- and four-part fugues, and could have been combined with the original subject in parallel thirds;

9) The tied note ending motive (2) and starting motive (3) in the original subject is frequently part of the structure of combining motives. The length of the tie most frequently is determined by the time span required to resolve the first motive before beginning

the momentum of the second motive.

THE EXPOSITION

Each of the structures for the expositions in
Die Kunst der Fuge could be used for other fugue types
or with varying subjects to produce a fugue structure
other than that presented in Die Kunst der Fuge by Bach.

THE COUNTER-SUBJECTS

The structure of the counter-subjects can vary from
real, tonal, and free throughout the fugue or in the
exposition, to "migrating" counter-subjects. In fugues
with more than one subject, any one subject can serve
as a counter-subject to another subject. New motives
in the counter-subject can add another dimension of
contrast to the subject, and lead to ingenious motivic
expansion in the episodes and free material.

THE EPISODES AND THEIR DEVELOPMENT

The episodes can vary from simple transitional
passages between statements of the subject or major
sections, to independent structures. A study of the
descriptions given in Chapter Four of the treatment of
the episodes in the individual fugues in Die Kunst der
Fuge reveals the contrapuntal potential of this component of the fugue form.

No two fugues have exactly the same process of
episodic development, and each fugue incorporates at
least one new example of motivic expansion. By extending
the length of an episode or adding a voice, one episode
can serve a climactic function, as in Episode (6) of
Contrapunctus I. Without reducing the number of voices,
numerous rests can separate motives in an episode to
reduce the tension, as in Episodes (5) and (6) in
Contrapunctus II. Episodes can present a contrasting
texture or provide the avenue for a traditional
historical convention, as the trio sonata episodes
in Contrapunctus III. Bach prepares the entrance of
the prevailing tradition in the first episode of this
same fugue. Contrapunctus IV would permit a study
of the structure of the episodes free from the fugal
thematic structure because the episodes are so
weighty and carefully expanded.

Canonic episodes serve the function of "intermediate episodes" in addition to the regular motivic
development of Contrapunctus V. The episodes embody

the French rhythmic thrust of Contrapunctus VI "in
Stile francese". The four episodes in Contrapunctus
VII separate the four statements of the subject in aug-
mentation, and separate the entire fugue into two units.

The episodes in the double and triple fugues illustrate the high level of motivic development that is made
possible by the usage of two or three subjects in one
fugue. Motivic imitation in normal order, in inversion,
augmentation, diminution, and mirror treatment all are
a standard part of the imitative devices used for the
motives. Four voices can be individually sequential,
resulting in imitation in pairs. Key relationships
can produce cycles of fifths or transient modulations
in the episodes to add to the color or climactic implications. A new chromatic motive can add harmonic and
contrapuntal variation to a section or the presentation of a new subject, as in Episodes (3) to (6) in
Contrapunctus XI. Numerous tied notes can temporarily
suspend the movement for lightened tension, as in
Episode (18) in Contrapunctus XI.

Two upper parts can proceed as a duo, as in Episode
(1) of Contrapunctus XVI, over a third lower voice in a
varying structure. The episodes help to establish the
ultimate eighth-note movement sought in the completion
of Contrapunctus XVII.

In Contrapunctus XVIII the overlapping cadences in
the episodes permit a constant series of transient
modulations.

MOTIVIC EXPANSION

The episodes are completed by varying usages
of motives resulting in singular treatment of motivic
expansion in each fugue. The motivic scores reveal
this distinctive feature of motivic combination of each
fugue.

The Four Simple Fugues

Contrapunctus I:

1) The motives from the subject and the new
motive from the counter-subject are combined in chain
formation, i.e., the last note of every motive frequently serves as the first note of a new motive;

2) Individual motives from the subject and
counter-subject are stated in normal order, or inverted,

337

augmented, diminished, or extended;

3) One motive may be stated in varying ways simultaneously: Episode (1) in the bass has a continuous expanded usage of CS(1). The S and T extend CS(1) by adding a skip of a fourth from the inversion of Sub. (1), and extending the duration of the second note of the interval of a fourth. The S and T proceed by canon. This procedure of a two-part canon over a constantly moving third voice, all based on CS(1) is used later in the fugue, as in Episode (3). A contraction of one of the canonic voices occurs in Episode (4);

4) Larger intervallic leaps are used for climax in CS(1) in Episode (6).

Contrapunctus II:

1) Since the motives from the CS can be said to be taken from the subject in this fugue, the episodes and free material are essentially taken from the subject. Bach uses the motives from the subject in a special way, dependent upon the "migrating" idea of the CS. Just as the CS is frequently stated first in one voice and then another, so are the motives in the episodes stated in constantly changing voices. A primary example of this statement of motives in varying voices can be seen in Episode (3); in fact, these voices state the motive in circular fashion;

2) Free voices frequently combine with the motives of the CS, or imitate these motives in normal order, in inversion, or mirror imitation, or paired voices.

Contrapunctus III:

1) Bach frequently alternates the chromatic CS(1) with a motive of the subject, as can be seen in Episodes (2), (4) and (5) the upper voices resulting in a chromatic contrapuntal style. The statement of the chromatic CS(1) as the last motive in an alternating sequence leads conveniently to the next statement of the CS, as in Ms. 42-43, in the A;

2) The omission of the principle of alternation of motives as chromatic counterpoint is compensated by chromatic harmonies in Episode (6).

Contrapunctus IV:

1) By retaining a four-voice texture in many
of the episodes, each voice can continue by sequence
and two voices can be combined in imitation in pairs;

2) When the voices no longer proceed by imitation in pairs and all voices retain their own motivic
identity, as in Episode (3), Ms. 47-52, a dissolution
of the motives occurs giving the effect of climactic
increased tension within the episode;

3) One motive being imitated by all voices, as
at the start of Episode (6), affords another gradation
of climax at this juncture in the fugue.

The Three Stretto Fugues

The tight statements of the subjects and answers
with no counter-subjects would seem to overshadow
attention to motivic development and expansion in the
episodes. This is not a necessary limitation.

Contrapunctus V: Each of the episodes has a
slightly different motivic structure:

> Episode (1) - paired imitation;
> (2) - imitation between three
> voices;
> (3) - two paired voices with con-
> stant dissonant and con-
> sonant voices, above a
> moving bass;
> (4) - voices in paired imitation,
> then dissolved;
> (5) - canonic imitation (quadruple);
> (6) - three voices in imitation,
> followed by inverted can-
> onic imitation (quadruple);
> (7) - each voice sequential, par-
> tially imitative; and
> (8) - increased new material, with
> added chromaticism.

Contrapunctus VI:

1) The omitted voice in the episodes varies
the dynamic coloration of the fugue, i.e., the omitted
T in Episode (1) creates a darker color than the
higher-ranged three-voice Episode (2), Ms. 12-1/2 to
15, with B omitted;

2) The number of appearances of the

thirty-second note figures creates varying weights of tension in the episodes;

3) Rests between motives give a feeling of relaxed tension in the first part of Episode (3) in Div. Two, contrasting with the new drive of melodic energy starting with M. 54-1/2 in the same episode.

Contrapunctus VII:

1) Larger skips within motives and increased chromaticism in Episodes (2) and (4) divide this complex stretto fugue into two units. The climactic significance of Episode (2) is introduced by the higher range, chromatic counterpoint, and intervallic leaps back in M. 24 in the B;

2) The type of motivic construction in the free voices in this tightly-woven stretto fugue depends upon the voices stated in stretto;

3) Although imitation exists primarily in the free voices, some imitation by diminution of motives from the subject occurs within the same measures;

4) Episode (2) shows imitation between the two upper voices; Episode (4) shows melodic concentration on an added upper fifth voice, with some imitation in the next two lower voices.

The Double and Triple Fugues

Contrapunctus VIII:

The greatest motivic complexity exists in the two triple fugues, Contrapunctus VIII and Contrapunctus XI.

1) The first episode, as in several previous fugues, sets the conditions for the subsequent motivic procedures;

2) One voice can expand motives from the Sub. or CS, while the remaining voice(s) can alternate motives from the Sub. and CS;

3) A combination of motives from the Sub. and CS can be used in sequence, or in various imitative patterns;

4) Bach introduces the third subject by

referring to motives from this subject before it appears;

5)   The three subjects are so planned that the tie at the beginning of Sub. II can be used to combine motives, as in Episode (17). Because of the rhythmic alteration of Sub. III, based on the original subject, the tie is omitted from Sub. III;

6)   The chromatic implications in Sub. II permit combination with chromatic motive ISub.(1c);

7)   Transient modulations in Episode (14), based on constantly changing motives, climactically introduce the first statement of the three subjects in triple counterpoint.

Contrapunctus IX:

1)   Imitation of motives from Sub. I retaining a constant eighth-note movement is the chief concern of the motives, especially in the episodes;

2)   Paired imitation of ISub.(4) in augmentation is stated in Episode (5), above a moving third voice;

3)   Two voices moving in parallel or complementary eighth-note movement add climax to the eighth-note imitation.

Contrapunctus X:

1)   Motives from Sub. II are not introduced before the entrance of Sub. II;

2)   The fugal entrance of motives entering in a cycle of fifths is an innovation appearing in Episode (6) of this fugue. This fugal entry permits a closing of Sec. IVB and the entrance of Sec. IVC. A similar idea was begun in M. 22 in the bass directly preceding Div. Two. The same procedure for introducing new statements in double counterpoint is found in Ms. 101-103, and the inverted motives are partially used to introduce the last double counterpoint statement in Ms. 111-115;

3)   The fragmented bass sequence in Episode (7) creates a partially-dark color;

4)   The tightness of the motives in imitation

by all voices determines the tension of the episodes.

Contrapunctus XI:

1) ISub.(3) is emphasized in Episode (1-B) in Ms. 18-1/4 to 22. ISub.(3a) is further almost consistently stated in some form of imitation, ending in three voices stating ISub.(3) in parallel motion;

2) The Chr. M. surrounding Sub. II permits chromatic joining of motives;

3) Rests relieve the tension in chromatically dense sections;

4) All four voices stating motives from Sub. III simultaneously create contrasting intermediate sections;

5) When one subject is stated in mirror counterpoint, as in Sec. XI, the remaining voices draw upon motives of the same subject or contrasting subjects.

The Two Mirror Fugues

Contrapunctus XVI:

1) A trio texture contrasts with duo sections combined with pedal point. The duo sections exist with free voices, or between one free voice and the statement of a subject or answer;

2) Episodes (2) and (4) have the most intricate imitatively independent sections;

3) Episode (3) has a dramatically dense interplay of short motives with new material.

Contrapunctus XVII:

1) Imitative passages with an increasing usage of eighth notes gradually create a consistent eighth-note background;

2) The eighth-note motivic structure in all four voices is climactically the most dense in Episode (6).

The Quadruple Fugue

Contrapunctus XVIII:

1) Div. One and Expo. II use only motives from Sub. I and Sub. II, respectively, or an occasional new motive;

2) Not until Sub. I is stated in double counterpoint with Sub. II in Sec. IX are motives from both subjects combined;

3) Motives from Sub. II are emphasized in all of Div. Two;

4) Motives from Sub. III are emphasized in all of Division Three.

THE FREE MATERIAL

Because the episodes together with the free material in many of the fugues seem equally as vital to the structure of the entire fugue as the statements of the subjects and answers, an analysis of the free material as separate from the episodes in one fugue will illustrate the significance of this material. Contrapunctus IV has been selected for this study.

Sec. I, Ms. 11-19 (Exposition, Ms. 1-19). The S and A in M. 11 continue the motivic sequences begun in Episode (1). The A anticipates the CS in M. 12. The descending third motive is first stated in the free S voice in Ms. 14-3/4 to 17. At this juncture in the fugue where the descending third motive is not heard in imitation, but rather by sequence in one voice, the relationship of this third to the two successive ascending third intervals in the B answer can be seen. The S then continues in imitation of the A. The A introduces the first measure of the CS in 14-1/2, so that the statement of the CS by the T seems in imitation of the A CS motive.

Sec. II, Ms. 27 to 43-1/2.

Sec. IIA, Ms. 27-31. S states Sub.; A has reference to CS. Imitation exists between A and T in Ms. 29-30, and the B has an ascending chromatic bass line.

Sec. IIB, Ms. 31-35. A states Sub.; no CS is included. The S imitates one descending third motive stated by the B. The remaining free material is partially sequential.

343

Sec. IIC, Ms. 35-39. T states Sub.; A states CS. The S begins a sequence based on the descending third, but then cadences. The B is silent.

Sec. IID, Ms. 39 to 43-1/2. B states Sub.; T has references to CS on contrasting beats. The imitation between the S and A leads directly to Episode (3). The constantly changing imitative passages between the S and A seem to be expanded in Episode (3). From M. 40-1/4 to M. 45, the S and A are first imitative, based on the third descending; then imitation in mirror order; imitation in normal order; and imitation in inversion. The S and A are paired in the first part of Episode (3), with the T and B joining in paired imitation following their statements of the CS and Sub., respectively.

Sec. III, Ms. 61-81.

Sec. IIIA, Ms. 61-65. B states Sub.; S and A state CS in imitation for several measures, then A anticipates the S CS in M. 65.

Sec. IIIB, Ms. 65-69. T states Sub.; A and S continue in imitation based on the CS(1). After this imitative passage, the S ends until M. 77 when the S enters as Sub. The B proceeds by sequence, leading directly to Episode (4).

Sec. IIIC, Ms. 73-77. A states Sub.; T has reference to CS on contrasting beats, then proceeds partially sequential. The B begins sequential, then proceeds freely to its cadence in M. 77. The S is omitted.

Sec. IIID, Ms. 77-81. S states Sub,; A has reference to CS on contrasting beats, with added motives similar to T in Sec. IIIC. T and B proceed in paired imitation using descending third motive, and then continue to Episode (5).

Sec. IV, Ms. 107-115.

Sec. IVA, Ms. 107-111. The paired imitation between the S and A, as appeared in Secs. IIIA and IIIB, is now combined with the stretto statement of the Sub. by the T and B. Following one joint statement of the descending third motive in M. 110, the S and A continue with their stretto Ans. in M. 111.

Sec. IVB, Ms. 111-115. The paired voices are interchanged from Sec. IVA. The imitation between the

T and B continues for a short time, followed by a brief pedal point in the B in M. 113 to emphasize the conclusion of the two stretto statements.

Sec. V, Coda, Ms. 129-138.

Sec. VA, Ms. 129-133. T states modified Sub.; no CS is included. The B begins with one measure pedal point to emphasize the beginning of the coda, stating the tonic of the G Minor chord. The B then continues partially sequential with unusually large intervals in its motives. The S and A are freely paired.

Sec. VB, Ms. 133-137(138). A states Sub.; T and S have reference to CS. The S begins in M. 132-1/2 by imitating the motives previously stated by the B in Ms. 130 and 131. From M. 134, S and T are paired, first in mirror imitation, then in rhythmic imitation. The B has a lengthy pedal point beginning in M. 135 to the end.

NEW MATERIAL

The new material as indicated in the motivic score, is sparse in Die Kunst der Fuge. The usage of new material augments gradations of climax.

The new material adds:

1) ornamented notes to a given motive;

2) exaggerated skips to a pre-existing motive, or as a new motive;

3) chromaticism to one voice part;

4) numerous pedal point passages;

5) climactic cadential passages;

6) octave leaps;

7) trills;

8) motives that tend to dissolve a sequence of motives from a Sub. or CS, or motives that create a change or transition from one motivic idea to a new motivic idea;

9) rhythmically-altered motives;

10) rhythmic figurations; and

11) motivic contrast, by occasionally alter-
       nating new motives with motives of a
       Sub. or CS.

THE CODAS

No two codas are exactly the same in Die Kunst der
Fuge. They vary in function to a summation of ideas,
an expanded recapitulation, to a simple relaxation of
tension.

IN CONCLUSION, all aspects of Die Kunst der Fuge
are additive. To add new procedures to fugal construction is the primary goal of Bach in writing this compendium. Bach illustrates his ideologies in meticulously crafted fugues with music of the highest quality.
Bach proves that each component of the fugue form,
whether it be the fugue type or overall structure, or
whether it be the subject(s), counter-subject, episodes,
free material, motivic expansion, new material, or
coda, or the presentation of a new subject in its
appropriate exposition, contributes to the final completed fugue in an individual way. By a thoughtful
study of the function of these aspects of fugal construction, no two fugues need ever be written exactly
the same, nor need they be bound by prevailing harmonic interests, contrapuntal limitations, nor a specific theoretical concept.

B I B L I O G R A P H Y

ORIGINAL SOURCES

Bach, Johann Sebastian, Die Kunst der Fuge.
Autograph in the Staatsbibliothek in Berlin
(microfilm).

EDITIONS

OPEN SCORE (with no keyboard reduction)

Bitsch, Marcel, J. S. Bach, L'Art de la Fugue.
Paris: Durand et Cie, Editeurs, 1967.

Gal, Hans, J. S. Bach, Die Kunst der Fuge, ...
Hawkes Pocket Scores. London, New York:
Boosey & Hawkes, Ltd., 1951.

Lea Pocket Scores, J. S. Bach, Die Kunst der Fuge
(The Art of the Fugue). L.P.S. No. 73. (From
the Bach-Gesellschaft Edition, edited by
Wilhelm Rust). New York, 1955.

Rust, Wilhelm, Bach-Gesellschaft, Vol. 25. Leipzig,
1878.

Tovey, Sir Donald Francis, Die Kunst der Fuge (The
Art of Fugue) by Johann Sebastian Bach (edited
and completed with a dissertation). London:
Oxford University Press, 1923.

OPEN SCORE (with keyboard reduction)

Graeser, Wolfgang, Neuen Bachgesellschaft, Jg.
XXVIII, Heft 1. Leipzig: Breitkopf & Härtel,
1927.

Kalmus Miniature Orchestra Scores, Johann Sebastian
Bach, The Art of the Fugue, No. 180. New
York: Edwin F. Kalmus.

ORCHESTRA

Graeser, Wolfgang, Die Kunst der Fuge. Leipzig:
Breitkopf & Härtel.

Vuataz, Roger, Die Kunst der Fuge. Zurich:
Hermann Scherchen-Ars Viva, 1950.

(EDITIONS, continued)

ORGAN

Schurich, Hans, Die Kunst der Fuge, Teile I and II,
    newly revised by Bruno Penzien. Heidelberg:
    Willy-Müller Suddeutscher Musikverlag,
    1944-1952.

Walcha, Helmut, Johann Sebastien Bach, Die Kunst
    der Fugue, The Art of the Fugue. Henry
    Litolff's Verlag. New York: C. F. Peters,
    1967.

PIANO

Czerny, Carl, reduced for Piano by, Johann
    Sebastian Bach, the Art of the Fugue. Kalmus
    Piano Series. New York: Edwin F. Kalmus.

Czerny, Carl, Bach, Die Kunst der Fuge. Edition
    Peters Nr. 218 (9680). New York: C. F. Peters
    Corp.

Husman, Dr. Heinrich, Joh. Seb. Bach, Die Kunst der
    Fuge. Leipzig: Steingräber Verlag, 1938.

STRING QUARTET

Harris, Roy, and M. D. Herter Norton, Johann
    Sebastian Bach, The Art of the Fugue.
    New York: G. Schirmer, Inc., 1936.

BOOKS, ARTICLES, MISCELLANEOUS SCORES

Apel, Willi, "Bachs Kunst der Fuge" in Die Musik,
    XXII, 1930.

Bridge, J. Frederick, Double Counterpoint and Canon.
    New York: H. W. Gray Co., Inc., 1881.

Busoni, Ferruccio, Fantasia Contrappuntistica für
    Klavier in drei Fassungen. Nr. 3491. Leipzig:
    Breitkopf & Härtel, 1910.

Bush, Douglas E., "J. S. Bach's 'The Art of Fugue'"
    in Music, Vol. 8, No. 5, May, 1974.

Conze, Johannes, "Bachs Quadrupel-Fugen-Fragment"
    in Allgemeine Musik-Zeitung, 64, 1937.

(BOOKS, ARTICLES, MISCELLANEOUS SCORES, continued)

David, Hans T. and Arthur Mendel, The Bach Reader.
New York: W. W. Norton & Company, Inc., 1945
(1966).

David, Hans T., "Kritischer Anhang: Zu Bachs
'Kunst der Fuge'" in Jahrbuch der Musikbiblio-
thek Peters, XXXIV, 1927.

Fux, J. J. Gradus ad Parnassum, in Monuments of
Music and Music Literature in Facsimile, Second
Series - Music Literature XXIV, Vienna, 1725.
New York: Broude Brothers, 1966.

Fux, J. J., Gradus ad Parnassum (Steps to Parnassus:
The Study of Counterpoint), translated and
edited by Alfred Mann with the collaboration
of John St. Edmunds. New York: W. W. Norton &
Company, Inc., 1943.

Gräser, Wolfgang, "Bachs 'Kunst der Fuge'" in
Bach Jahrbuch, 1924.

Harris, Roy, and M. D. Herter Norton, "The Art of
the Fugue" in The Musical Quarterly, XXI,
Nr. 2, 1935.

Hauptmann, Moritz, Erläuterungen zu J. S. Bachs
Kunst der Fuge, Leipzig, New York: C. F.
Peters, 1841, 1861. Neue, unveränderte Aus-
gabe 1881 u. 1925.

Husman, Heinrich, "Die 'Kunst der Fuge' als
Klavierwerk" in Bach Jahrbuch, 1938.

Keller, Wilhelm, "Das Thema von Bachs 'Kunst der
Fuge'" in Österr. Musik-Ztschr., Jg. 2, 1947.

Kitson, C. H., Invertible Counterpoint and Canon.
London: Oxford University Press, 1927.

Leonhardt, Gustav M., The Art of Fugue, Bach's Last
Harpsichord Work, An Argument. The Hague:
Martinus Nijhoff, 1952.

Mann, Alfred, The Study of Fugue. New Brunswick,
New Jersey: Rutgers University Press, 1958.

Marpurg, Friedrich Wilhelm, Hist.-Krit. Beyträge
zur Aufnahme der Musik, 5 Vols., 1754-1772.

(BOOKS, ARTICLES, MISCELLANEOUS SCORES, continued)

Marpurg, Friedrich Wilhelm, Abhandlung von der Fuge.
   Wien, 1729.

Martin, Bernhard, "Zwei Durchfuhrungsmodi der
   Tripelfuge zum Fragment aus der 'Kunst der
   Fuge' von Johann Sebastian Bach" in Bach
   Jahrbuch, 1940/48.

Müller, Fritz, "Bachs 'Kunst der Fuge' für
   Tasteninstrumente" in Neue Ztschr. f. Musik,
   Jg. 97, 1930.

Playford, John, Introduction to the Skill of Music,
   in 3 Books. London: Printed by William
   Godbid, 1666.

Riemann, Hugo, "Gehort die 'unvollende' B-A-C-H
   Fuge zur 'Kunst der Fuge' oder nicht?" in
   Allgem. Musik-Ztg., XXI, 1894.

Rietsch, Heinrich, "Zur 'Kunst der Fuge' von
   J. S. Bach im Auftrage der Neuen Bachgesell-
   schaft herausgegeben von Arnold Schering" in
   Bach Jahrbuch, 1926.

Schlötterer-Traemir, Roswitha, Johann Sebastian
   Bach, Die Kunst der Fuge. München: Wilhelm
   Fink Verlag, 1966.

Schumann, Robert. "Uber einige mutmasslich
   corrumpierte Stellen in Bach'schen,
   Mozart'schen und Beethoven'schen Werken" in
   Neue Ztsch. für Musik, Jg. 38, December 9,
   1841.

Schwebsch, Erich, Joh. Seb. Bach und die Kunst der
   Fuge. Stuttgart, den Haag, London: Orient-
   Occident-Verlag, 1931.

Stauffer, George, "Bach's 'Art of Fugue' An
   Examination of the Sources" in Current
   Musicology, Number 19/1975.

Tenschert, Roland, "'Die Kunst der Fuge' von Johann
   Sebastian Bach" in Österreichische Musik-
   Zeitschrift, Jg. 1, Heft 1, 1946.

Terry, Charles Sanford, "Bach's Swan-Song" in The
   Musical Quarterly, XIX, No. 3, July 1933.

(BOOKS, ARTICLES, MISCELLANEOUS SCORES, continued)

Theile, Johann, Musicalisches Kunstbuch, in
        Denkmäler Norddeutscher Music, Band I, BA 5491.
        New York: Bärenreiter (Kassel), 1965.

Tovey, D. F., A Companion to 'The Art of Fugue',
        London: Humphrey-Milford; Oxford University
        Press, 1931.

Walther, Johann Gottfried, Praecepta der
        Musicalischen Composition, Caput 10, "De
        Fugis", Herausgegeben vor Peter Benary.
        Leipzig: Breitkopf & Härtel, 1955.

Waltz, Hermann, "Zur Erganzung der Quadrupel Fuge
        aus Bachs 'Kunst der Fuge' durch K. H.
        Pillney", in Allgem, Musik-Ztg., 64, 1937.

Ziehn, B., "Gehort die 'unvollendete' Bachfuge zur
        'Kunst der Fuge' oder nicht?" in Allgem.
        Musik-Ztg., XXI, Nr. 33/34, 1894.